CW01631613

Incredibly Interesting Science Facts For Smart Kids

Think You Know Science? Think Again! —

Here are 999+ Fascinating Science Facts: Mind-Blowing Discoveries & Inventions from Around the World

Petite Dreamer

© Copyright 2025 - All rights reserved.

The content contained within this book may not be reproduced, duplicated or transmitted without direct written permission from the author or the publisher.

Under no circumstances will any blame or legal responsibility be held against the publisher, or author, for any damages, reparation, or monetary loss due to the information contained within this book, either directly or indirectly.

Legal Notice:

This book is copyright protected. It is only for personal use. You cannot amend, distribute, sell, use, quote or paraphrase any part, or the content within this book, without the consent of the author or publisher.

Disclaimer Notice:

Please note the information contained within this document is for educational and entertainment purposes only. All effort has been executed to present accurate, up to date, reliable, complete information. No warranties of any kind are declared or implied. Readers acknowledge that the author is not engaged in the rendering of legal, financial, medical or professional advice. The content within this book has been derived from various sources. Please consult a licensed professional before attempting any techniques outlined in this book.

By reading this document, the reader agrees that under no circumstances is the author responsible for any losses, direct or indirect, that are incurred as a result of the use of the information contained within this document, including, but not limited to, errors, omissions, or inaccuracies.

Special Bonus

I sincerely thank you for taking the time to read my book! We are exclusively providing the PDF of *"Incredibly Interesting Global Facts For Smart Kids"* free of charge.

https://pubbooklist.com/sci-fact

Readers have reported the following side effects:

- Uncontrollable Smiling – in response to every warm "hello" from around the globe!
- Joyful Tears – triggered by ancient landmarks sharing their untold stories!
- An Impulsive Desire to Discover – as the world beckons you!
- Yearnings for Global Tastes – your kitchen could transform into a cultural hub!
- Time-Traveling Fantasies – each chapter transports you through history!

Enjoy your free sample audiobook!

Are you interested in a complimentary audiobook of "Incredibly Interesting Science Facts For Smart Kids"? Access it below.

https://youtu.be/oW_Lj8cIqXI

If you're curious about the complete audiobook, please see the information below or contact me directly via email.

https://pubbooklist.com/sci-fact

kate@pubbooklist.com

Thank You

If you love our brand, make sure to visit our **brand page** for more exciting content!

https://www.amazon.com/stores/author/B0CKVJYFDB

You had plenty of books available, but you chose this one—thank you! I'm grateful for your dedication to reading it completely. Before you go, I have a small favor to ask: could you write a review on the platform? Your review is one of the easiest and most impactful ways to support independent authors like myself. Your feedback will help me create books that can assist you in reaching your goals. It really means a lot to hear from you.

US: https://www.amazon.com/review/create-review/?asin=B0F2H3CYCF

UK: https://www.amazon.co.uk/review/create-review/?asin=B0F2H3CYCF

CA: https://www.amazon.ca/review/create-review/?asin=B0F2H3CYCF

TABLE OF CONTENTS

INTRODUCTION

"Research shows that even brief, daily science sessions can boost creativity and problem-solving skills by over 60%!"

Picture a world where every 7-minutes you're catapulted into a new realm of scientific wonder—from the vast cosmos to the tiniest cell!

Picture a book that has pages filled with a lot of colorful knowledge and facts about everything — from animals to the sun!

What if science could bridge cultures and spark creativity in every language? What if science could be learned in small, interactive bits that never get boring?

Imagine yourself exploring the secrets of the stars, the oceans, and our universe! Welcome to a book that makes science fun, easy to understand, and full of exciting global discoveries!

Why Does Science Matter?

Science is more than just experiments and formulas—it's a universal language that connects us all. No matter where you are in the world, or what language you speak, the laws of physics, the wonders of biology, and the mysteries of the universe remain the same.

Did you know that the number zero was first developed by mathematicians in ancient India, or that Chinese scientists invented the first seismometer over 1,800 years ago to measure earthquakes? These are just some of the incredible ways different cultures have contributed to science!

Throughout history, people from all parts of the world have observed nature, experimented with materials, and developed technologies that changed the way we live.

The Mayans studied the movement of planets and stars, creating a calendar more accurate than the one used in Europe at the time.

African metallurgists were among the first to master ironwork, long before it became common in other parts of the world.

Science is everywhere—it is a gift from human curiosity and ingenuity. It is a gift to you and me!

This book will take you on an adventure through some of the most amazing facts about our world and beyond. Each chapter is designed to be fun, engaging, and easy to read, even if you only have a few minutes a day. Whether you're curious about space, animals, inventions, or the human body, there's something here for you.

Science in Every Language

If you speak more than one language or live in a multilingual home, you may have noticed that different languages describe the same scientific ideas in different ways. In Korean, the word for "science" (과학, gwahak) means "the study of rules," while in Spanish, (ciencia) comes from the Latin word for knowledge. This should tell you that no matter the language, science is about asking questions and discovering answers. And that is what this book will help you to do.

This book will introduce you to famous scientists from around the world and show how their discoveries shaped the way we live today. Have you ever heard of Katherine Johnson, the African American mathematician whose calculations helped NASA send astronauts to the Moon? Or Ibn al-Haytham, the Arab scientist who made early discoveries about how we see light? Their stories prove that great science happens everywhere and with the help of everyone!

And science isn't just something you find in books or labs—it's part of everyday life! When you boil water, play with magnets, or watch a rainbow appear after the rain, you're witnessing science in action. Science helps us to understand our world and offers the necessary tools to enrich it.

Why I Wrote This Book

I'm Petite Dreamer, and I grew up in a multilingual, multicultural family. My roots are in two continents and, as an adult, I have lived in five other cities in four different countries across the world, where I've met people from different cultures. I've always been fascinated by how different cultures and languages can come together to create something amazing.

As an educator, I've spent years working with kids just like you, helping them learn about science, languages, and cultures. I've seen how excited kids get when they discover something new, and I've made it my mission to create books that make learning fun and accessible for everyone.

This book is also inspired by my own experience as a parent. I know kids prefer to learn in interactive ways. So, I want to show you how science is a global adventure, with contributions from people of all cultures and backgrounds. Together, we'll explore the wonders of the universe, the Earth, animals, and even the human body.

How This Book Works

Each chapter in this book will introduce you to a new scientific topic, packed with fun facts, interesting experiments, and cool discoveries from different parts of the world. This book targets readers aged 8–12, especially those who enjoy text-heavy books and are naturally curious about science. Even adults who like light, approachable science topics might enjoy it!

Here's what to expect from the book:

- **Exciting Science Facts** from around the world and across different centuries.
- **Questions** that will make you think deeply, critically, and creatively about science.
- **Interactive Activities** and simple science experiments that you can do at home.
- **Scientist Spotlights** on the global pioneers who made history with their inventions.
- **Quick Summaries** at the end of each chapter, with key takeaways so you can remember the most important points.

Get Ready to Explore!

Science is all around us—from the stars in the sky to the tiniest atoms that make up everything we see.

You're holding the key to a world of engaging, bite-sized STEM adventures. Are you ready to go on a journey of discovery?

Dive in NOW and let your curiosity lead you to new horizons!

Flip the page and let's begin with our first chapter: Cosmic Wonders – The Universe Unveiled!

CHAPTER 1: Cosmic Wonders – The Universe Unveiled

"We are made of star stuff. We are a way for the universe to know itself" – Carl Sagan

"How do countless stars and galaxies tell the story of our existence?"

Section 1: The Vastness of Space

Have you ever wondered how far the stars are from us? The universe is so big that it's hard to even imagine! But don't worry—we're going to break it down into bite-sized pieces.

Sub-section 1.1: Understanding Cosmic Distances

What makes up our solar system?

1. Our sun and the eight planets that orbit the sun are the major components of our solar system

Can you write down the names of the eight planets in our solar system?

2. They are Mercury, Venus, Earth, Mars, Jupiter, Saturn, Uranus and Neptune.

3. Jupiter is the largest planet and its diameter is eleven times that of our planet.

4. To compare, the sun's diameter is ten times that of Jupiter.

Why is Pluto not a planet?

5. Pluto used to be considered a planet. So your parents may still think of it that way.

6. But actually, Pluto is a dwarf planet that does not meet all the rules to be called a regular planet (like the other ones we listed above).

7. There are five official dwarf planets in our solar system: Pluto, Eris, Ceres, Makemake, and Haumea.

8. Our moon isn't the only moon in our solar system. How many moons do you think are in our solar system?

9. **293** moons! One moon for Earth; two for Mars; 95 at Jupiter; 146 at Saturn; 28 at Uranus; 16 at Neptune; and five for dwarf planet Pluto.

What do you know about the Milky Way Galaxy?

10. Earth and our solar system is located in the The Milky Way, but we are nit the only planet in this massive galaxy.

11. The Milky Way Galaxy also contains billions of other stars, planets, and cosmic objects.

12. The Milky Way Galaxy is also only one of the countless galaxies in the universe.

What are cosmic distances?

13. Cosmic distances are the huge spaces between objects in space. Think about the distance from your home to school. Now imagine that distance stretched out millions or even billions of times!

Since cosmic distances are huge, how do we measure them?

14. Scientists use the special units, light-years, parsecs, and astronomical units (AU) to measure the distances between stars, galaxies and within our solar system respectively. Let's find out what these mean!

What is a light-year and why do scientists use it to measure cosmic distances?

15. A light-year is the distance that light travels in one year.

And guess what?

16. Light is super fast—it zooms through space at about 300,000 kilometers (186,000 miles) per second!

17. That means that in just one second, light could travel around the Earth 7.5 times. Now, imagine how far light could go in a whole year. That's a light-year!

18. Scientists use light-years because cosmic distances are larger than the usual units of distance like miles and kilometers.

Is one light-year really that big?

19. A resounding Yes! For example, the closest star to Earth (after the Sun) is called Proxima Centauri, and it's about 4.24 light-years away.

20. The light we see from Proxima Centauri today actually left the star over 4 years ago! Awesome!

Parsecs are even bigger than light-years

21. One parsec is about 3.26 light-years. Scientists use parsecs to measure distances between stars and galaxies.

22. The center of our Milky Way galaxy is about 8,000 parsecs away from us. That's about 27,000 light years away. That's so far that even light takes tens of thousands of years to travel that distance! Wow, right?

23. Astronomical Units (AU) are used for measurement within our solar system. One AU represents the distance from the Earth to the Sun, a span of roughly 93 million miles).

24. That distance is the equivalent of going from Rosario in Argentina to Xinghua in China **7,300** times.

25. Jupiter is about 5.2 AU from the Sun, meaning it's 5.2 times farther from the Sun than Earth is.

What's the farthest thing you can see in the night sky?

26. On a very clear night, you might see the Andromeda Galaxy. This galaxy is approximately 2.5 million light-years away.

27. The light you'd see left Andromeda 2.5 million years ago—around the time early humans were just starting to walk on Earth!

Interactive Activity: Create Your Own Solar System Scale Model

Let's get hands-on! Here's a fun activity to help you understand cosmic distances.

Get a large open space (like a park or playground). Place a large ball at one end of the space to represent the Sun. Place Earth (a small bead) 15 meters (50 feet) away from the Sun.

Place Jupiter (a marble) 80 meters (260 feet) away and Pluto (a tiny speck) 600 meters (2,000 feet) away. If the playground is not big enough for Pluto, imagine just how big our solar system is.

As you step back and look at your model, now remember that our solar system is located in the corner of our Galaxy, and there are billions, maybe trillions of galaxies in the Universe!

Sub-section 1.2: The Expanding Universe

Is the Universe growing?

28. Yes! The universe is expanding. Picture a balloon with dots on it. As you blow it up, the dots move apart because the balloon is growing bigger. That's what's happening to the universe.

Have you heard of Hubble's Law?

29. American astronomer Edwin Hubble was the first to discover that galaxies are moving away from us, proving that the universe is getting bigger.

What is Hubble's Law?

30. Hubble wrote Hubble's Law to explain this. He noticed that the farther away a galaxy is, the faster it seems to be moving away from us.

What is redshift?

31. As galaxies move farther away, the light they emit stretches into longer wavelengths, shifting toward the red part of the spectrum. That means that the light they emit appears reddish but you cannot see this with the naked eye.

How do astronomers measure redshift?

32. Astronomers use a spectrometer to analyze the spectrum of light from an object. That allows them to determine if they are shifted towards the red end of the spectrum, indicating a redshift.

What is the opposite of redshift?

33. The opposite of redshift is a blueshift which occurs when a body moves closer to us. Blueshifts are very rare in our solar system.

Interactive Activity: Timeline Quiz

Can you put these events in order, starting from the earliest to the most recent?

A. The Big Bang Happens

B. The first stars light up

C. Hubble discovers the universe is expanding

D. The Hubble Space Telescope is launched

Answer: The correct order is (A, B, C, D).

Did you get it right?

Sub-section 1.3: Tools for Cosmic Discovery

We can't hop into a car and drive to a star. So, we need amazing tools to study the stars, moons, and other planets.

34. The most common of the tools that are used by scientists to study the universe are telescopes, satellites, and space probes.

What was Galileo Galilei's contribution to astronomy?

35. In 1609, Galileo Galilei built one of the first telescopes, discovering moons around Jupiter and craters on the Moon.

36. The Hubble Telescope and James Webb Space Telescope are powerful telescopes that can be used to see billions of light years away.

What is the role of space probes?

37. Space probes, like Voyager 1 and 2, have traveled to the outer edges of our solar system, sending back interesting images and data.

38. Some solar probes can even leave our solar system.

39. The Parker Solar Probe is the fastest-moving object ever made by humans which travels at over 430,000 miles per hour as it orbits the Sun!

40. The Parker Solar Probe has made its closest approach to the Sun, reaching a distance of just 3.8 million miles from the Surface of the sun on December 24, 2024, . That's the closest we have come to the Sun.

41. The Parker Probe is safe from the sun's heat because it is coated in a special, reflective ceramic paint.

42. In 2015, *New Horizons* provided the first clear, close-up pictures of Pluto.

43. *Curiosity* and *Perseverance* are robotic rovers that explore the surface of Mars to analyze rocks, soil and the atmosphere.

44. *Pioneer 10* was the first space probe to cross the asteroid belt and make direct observations of Jupiter.

45. *Galileo* studied Jupiter and its moons, and discovered a subsurface ocean on Europa.

Interactive Activity: Making a Mini Telescope

To make a mini telescope, you will need two magnifying glasses. Hold one near your eye and the other at arm's length. Look through them to make far away things larger. That's how telescopes started before we developed the more powerful ones we have today!

Section 2: Celestial Mechanics and Phenomena

Space is not just big —it is also very busy. Planets orbit the sun, stars glow and fade, and entire galaxies are constantly in motion. What keeps everything in order?

Sub-section 2.1: The Dance of the Planets

Why do planets orbit the sun?

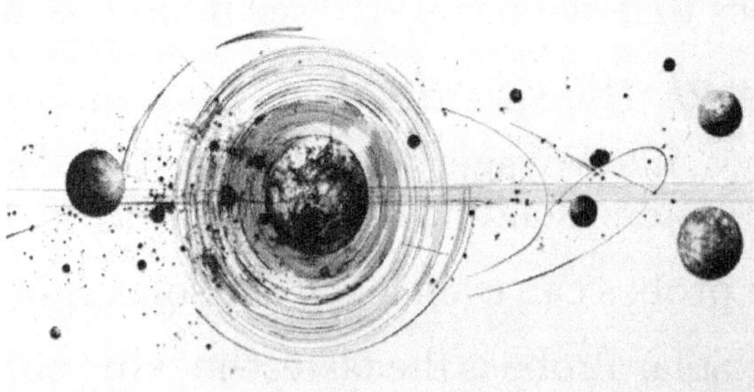

46. Have you ever spun a ball on a string? It keeps circling because you are pulling it. In space, gravity does the pulling and keeps the planets in place!

What are orbits?

47. Gravity pulls planets toward the Sun, but they are also moving forward through space, so they travel in curved paths called orbits. Each planet follows a specific orbit around the Sun.

Does each of the planets orbit the sun at the same speed?

48. Because of the differences in their distance from the sun, the orbits of each planet are not the same size.

49. Since they aren't of the same size, they're also not the same speed. Mercury races around the Sun in 88 days, while Neptune takes a slow 165 years!

Do moons have orbits too?

50. Yes. In the same way planets orbit the Sun, moons also orbit their specific planets. Earth's Moon takes about 27 days to circle us. The gravity of the Earth is what keeps the moon able to orbit around the Earth.

Who discovered that planets orbit the sun?

51. In the 16th century, Nicolaus Copernicus was the first to suggest the idea of orbital movement.

Why don't we feel the Earth moving?

52. Earth moves at about 107,000 km/h (67,000 mph), but we do not notice it because we're moving with it!

Interactive Activity: Simulating Orbital Motion

Tie a string to a small ball and swing it over your head. The string is gravity keeping the ball in orbit. Try it slow and fast—see how the force of the pull in your hand changes? What will happen if you let go of the string?

(Answer: The ball will fly off in a straight line. That's the same way planets and their moons would fall out of orbit if there were no gravity).

Sub-section 2.2: Stars, Galaxies, and Beyond

53. Just like living things such as plants and animals, stars have life cycles. They are born, grow, and eventually die.

How are stars formed?

54. Stars are born inside of large clouds of gas and dust known as nebulae. The gas and dust are pulled together and form a dense core, which then gets extremely hot.

How are galaxies formed?

55. Galaxies are huge collections of stars, gas, and dust held together by gravity.

56. The Milky Way is our galaxy and it contains billions of stars, including our Sun.

57. There are billions of galaxies out there in the universe. And even more universes out there as well!

What determines the life cycle of a star?

58. Its size! Small stars eventually expand into red giants and then shrink again to become white dwarfs.

What is a supernova?

59. Larger stars end their lives in spectacular explosions called supernovas, which can create new elements and even black holes.

What is a black hole?

60. A region of space where gravity is so strong that nothing, not even light, can escape is called a black hole.

61. Some black holes are millions of times heavier than our Sun, and scientists believe one lies at the center of our galaxy!

62. Our Sun has been shining for approximately 4.6 billion years.

63. The biggest star, "UY Scuti", can fit 5 billion Suns inside it!

64. In Japan, on July 7, people celebrate Tanabata, a festival about two stars meeting in the sky. It is a love story told by the stars.

Interactive Activity: The Life Cycle of a Star

Choose a known star (like Betelgeuse or Sirius) as a case study. Now, use the internet to find more information about your chosen star's life cycle. What stage is it in now? What do you think will happen to it in the future?

Sub-section 2.3: Interactive Cosmic Labs

We can recreate some cosmic phenomena in our laboratories.

Why should we recreate cosmic phenomena?

65. Studying cosmic phenomena on Earth helps scientists understand what is happening in space and the universe.

66. Scientists use experiments and simulations to study cosmic phenomena like black holes, supernovas, and even the Big Bang.

What are some famous interactive cosmic labs?

67. NASA's COSmIC Facility, NASA's Space Place and Hubble Online activities are some examples of Cosmic Labs.

68. These Cosmic Labs offer games, activities and videos that can help you to understand space.

Interactive Activity: Observing the Spread of a Supernova

You can try this at home! Creating a model of a supernova is easy. All you need is a piece of paper and a flashlight. Shine the flashlight through the paper and observe how the light spreads out, just like the explosion of a star.

Section 3: Global Scientist Spotlight – Astronomy Pioneers

Space would not make sense without the smart people who studied it. From ancient stargazers to today's explorers, they come from everywhere!

Sub-section 3.1: Trailblazers from Antiquity

Long before fancy tools, people watched the sky with their eyes and brains.

Did people study space before telescopes?

69. Yes, ancient astronomers from all over the world figured out a lot about the universe even without sophisticated tools.

70. As early as 1800 BCE, ancient astronomers in Babylon tracked stars on clay tablets.

71. In China, astronomers kept detailed records of comets and eclipses. In fact, centuries ago, Guo Shoujing built observatories to map the stars.

Who was Zhang Heng?

72. Zhang Heng was a Chinese astronomer and mathematician who was famous for making tools to watch the sky and exploding stars.

73. Zheng Heng invented the world's first water-powered armillary sphere for astronomical observation.

74. Zheng Heng also invented the world's first seismoscope, which is a tool for detecting the direction of an earthquake 500 km (310 mi) away.

75. Greek philosophers like Aristotle and Ptolemy were also instrumental in developing early models of the Universe.

76. Ptolemy was one of the first astronomers to suggest that the Earth was the center of the Universe. Later discoveries proved this wrong!

77. In India, Aryabhata was one of the earliest astronomers who studied planetary motion over 1,500 years ago.

Were there early female astronomers?

78. Yes. Hypatia was a famous Egyptian mathematician and one of the first known female astronomers.

79. Other notable early female astronomers were Émilie du Châtelet and Mary Somerville.

Sub-section 3.2: Modern Innovators in Astronomy

Modern astronomers have taken the study of the universe to new levels.

What have modern astronomers discovered?

80. Modern astronomers have discovered phenomena like black holes, exoplanets, and even the leftover heat from the Big Bang which is cosmic microwave background radiation.

81. Exoplanets are planets outside our solar system. They orbit other stars apart from the Sun.

82. Astronomers have discovered over 5,000 exoplanets including the Kepler-186f and Kepler-70b.

83. The Kepler-186f has Earth-like properties and exists in a habitable part of its solar system.

84. The Kepler-70b is the hottest exoplanet known with its temperature exceeding that of the sun.

Who are some famous modern astronomers?

85. Vera Rubin, an American astronomer, discovered dark matter, an invisible force that shapes galaxies.

86. Dr. Adriana Ocampo from Colombia found a crater showing where an asteroid hit Earth long ago.

87. Dr. Priyamvada Natarajan from India studies black holes and dark matter.

88. Subrahmanyan Chandrasekhar, an Indian-American astrophysicist, studied the life cycles of stars and won a Nobel Prize for his work.

89. In 2008, Dr. Takao Doi threw a specially designed boomerang into space. He was the first person to do this and he didn't just do it for fun. He threw it to see how boomerangs fly in zero gravity.

90. Carolyn Shoemaker was famous for discovering comets and asteroids. She discovered over 500 asteroids and 32 comets in her lifetime.

91. Isaac Newton is also famous for his work on gravity. He advanced theories about gravity after watching apples fall from a tree.

92. Stephen Hawking famously propounded that since the universe has a beginning, it will have an end. He also wrote the popular book, "A Brief History of Time."

93. Neil deGrasse Tyson is famous on television shows as a science educator and has written several books including, "The Pluto Files."

Interactive Activity: Looking Up A Modern Astronomer

Look up a modern astronomer that has not been named in this section. Read about them and their work. What are they famous for? How have they contributed to our understanding of the universe?

Sub-section 3.3: Inspiring Tomorrow's Explorers

Astronomy is a field that's open to everyone, no matter where you are from, the language you speak, or your age. The key ingredient to anything is curiosity and the boldness to ask big questions.

How can I become an astronomer?

94. You can join an astronomy club, attend star parties, or even participate in science competitions. Many universities offer programs in astronomy and astrophysics.

You don't need to be grown up to love or study space and our Universe. You can get started now!

Why not join an international astronomy club or participate in a global science competition? The universe is waiting for you to explore it!

Chapter Takeaways

- The Universe is vast, and scientists measure distances in parsecs, astronomical units and light years.
- The universe is always expanding and the galaxies within it are constantly moving away from each other.
- Telescopes, satellites, and space probes are valuable tools for exploring faraway stars and planets
- Gravity keeps planets orbiting the sun and stars live and die in cool ways.
- Scientists from everywhere, old and new, teach us about space.
- You can explore space with fun activities and clubs!

Are you ready for more wonders?

Chapter 2: Earth's Dynamic Landscape

"Our planet's surface is a mere skin over a dynamic, ever-changing interior!"

Have you ever wondered why mountains rise, earthquakes shake, and volcanoes erupt? What stories do these powerful forces tell about our planet?

Section 1: Plate Tectonics and Geological Forces

Did you know that Earth's surface is like a giant puzzle? But the pieces are constantly moving. These pieces are called tectonic plates, and they're responsible for shaping the world we live in.

Sub-section 1.1: The Shifting Crust

95. The surface of the Earth (the crust) is actually not solid. Instead, it is broken into giant pieces like a cracked eggshell.

96. These pieces float on a hot, semi-liquid layer called the mantle and move super slowly—about as fast as your fingernails grow!

97. Long ago, all the continents were part of one big landmass called Pangaea that existed about 300 million years ago, but they drifted apart over millions of years. That's called continental drift.

98. The continental drift explains why South America and Africa resemble puzzle pieces that could fit together.

99. In the early 1900s, Alfred Wegener became the first person to suggest the idea of continental drift. He did this after discovering that similar rocks and fossils were often found in different continents.

What is the origin of the name Pangaea?

100. Pangaea is of Greek origin and it means "All Earth." Pangaea was surrounded by a single ocean called Panthalassa.

Why do the tectonic plates move?

101. The plates move because heat from Earth's core swirls the mantle like a thick soup, pushing them around.

How fast do the plates move?

102. The plates move at different speeds, but on average, they move 2 to 5 centimeters per year. That may not seem like a lot at first, but remember that the plates have been moving for millions of years.

103. The fastest-moving plate is the Pacific Plate, which moves about 10 centimeters per year. That explains why places like California have so many earthquakes.

Can tectonic plates collide? What happens when they collide?

104. When plates collide, they can create mountains, cause earthquakes, or even form volcanoes.

105. The Himalayas are still growing taller today because the two plates (the Indian and the Eurasian) that formed it are actually still pushing together.

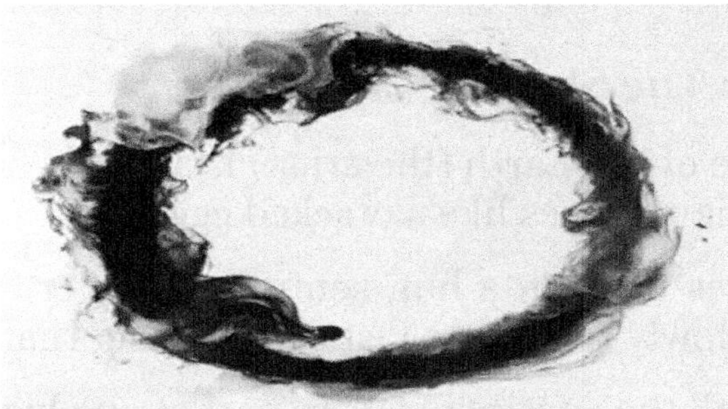

Have you heard of the Ring of Fire?

106. The Pacific Ring of Fire is a huge circular area of frequent volcanic eruptions and earthquakes around the Pacific Ocean where several plates meet.

107. The Ring of Fire is about 40,000 kilometers long and contains about two-thirds of all the volcanoes on Earth.

Interactive Activity: Tectonic Movement Maps and Models

Let's make a tectonic plate model!

1. Start with a hard-boiled egg. Now, carefully crack the shell. The cracked shell represents Earth's tectonic plates.
2. Now, gently push the pieces around - this is how the plates move over time.

Sub-section 1.2: Earthquakes and Seismic Activity

108. Sometimes, as tectonic plates try to slide past each other, they get stuck. Pressure continues to build up—like stretching a rubber band—until they snap free, causing an earthquake.

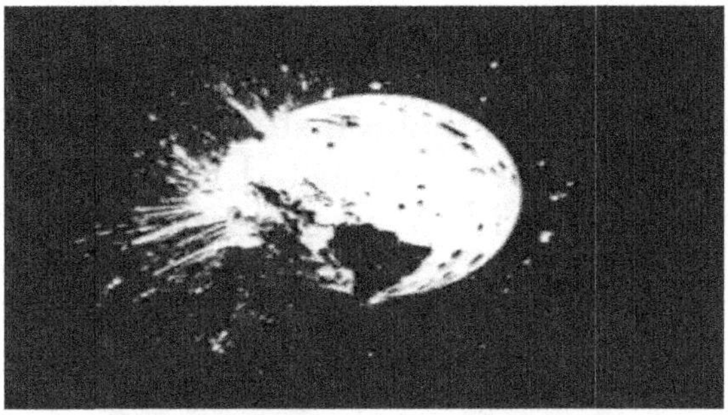

109. The spot underground where an earthquake starts is the focus and right above it, on the surface, is the epicenter.

110. Smaller earthquakes, called foreshocks, can precede the main earthquake.

111. Aftershocks, which can continue for days and even years, can follow the main earthquake

112. The Richter Scale measures the magnitude (strength) of an earthquake from 1 to 10.

113. The biggest earthquake ever recorded on the Richter Scale hit Chile in 1960 with a magnitude of 9.5!

114. Earthquakes are most likely to happen where plates meet, like along the San Andreas Fault in California.

115. The 1556 Shaanxi earthquake in China killed approximately 830,000 people and is considered the deadliest-ever!

What makes the ground shake during an earthquake?

116. Tectonic plates suddenly slip after being stuck, releasing energy that shakes everything!

Can animals feel earthquakes before us?

117. Maybe! Dogs and birds may sense the initial tiny shakes that humans miss.

118. Scientists can't predict exactly when an earthquake will happen, but they can identify areas where earthquakes are likely to occur.

Interactive Activity: Feeling a Quake

Rub two pieces of sandpaper together. Did you feel how they first stuck together due to friction? Then, they most likely slipped suddenly. That's how tectonic plates cause a quake!

Sub-section 1.3: The Birth of Mountains

Earth is filled with landmarks that tell stories of the different geological forces that the planet has been subjected to. From Saravejo to Cairo, scientists can read these stories. You can learn how to do it, too!

How do mountains develop?

119. Mountains develop when tectonic plates collide and push the earth's crust upwards. This process is called orogenesis.

120. Wind, water, and ice wear down the mountains in a process called erosion, creating valleys and shaping the landscape.

What is the tallest mountain in the world?

121. Mount Everest, in The Himalayas, is the tallest individual mountain peak in the world, standing at 8,848 meters (29,029 feet) above sea level.

122. Mount Everest is still growing at about 4 millimeters each year.

123. Mount Everest is so tall that its peak is in the 'death zone,' where there's not enough oxygen for humans to survive for long.

124. Climbers need special equipment to reach the top of Mountain Everest.

125. Sir Edmund Hilary and Tenzing Norgay were the first recorded people to reach the summit of Mt Everest on May 29, 1953.

126. In 2010, at just 13 years old, Jordan Romero became the youngest climber to reach the summit of Mt. Everest.

127. Yuichiro Miura of Japan is the oldest person to climb Mt Everest. He did it at the age of 80 in 2013.

128. Mauna Kea in Hawaii is taller than Mt Everest but starts on the ocean floor!

129. Mt Fuji and Mt Kilimanjaro, two famous mountains, are actually volcanoes.

130. Gangkhar Puensum in Bhutan is the highest unclimbed mountain in the world at 7,570 meters.

131. Climbing mountains above 6,000m is banned in Bhutan due to cultural and spiritual beliefs.

132. Mt Annapurna 1 is the deadliest mountain in the world with a fatality rate of 32% for climbers.

Section 2: Volcanic and Seismic Adventures

The Earth doesn't just move—it can also erupt and shake! Volcanoes and earthquakes are epic events that reshape our planet. Let us take a closer look at them.

Sub-section 2.1: The Fury of Volcanoes

Why do volcanoes erupt?

133. Volcanic eruption occurs when magma (hot, molten rock) rises to the surface from deep within the Earth. As magma rises, the pressure behind it builds up until the magma bursts through the Earth's crust, creating an eruption.

134. Some volcanoes explode violently, while others ooze lava slowly.

135. The Volcanic Explosivity Index, VEI, measures the power of volcanic eruptions.

Did you know?

136. The Romans give us the word 'volcano,' which is actually derived from Vulcan, who was their god of fire. The ancient Romans believed that volcanoes were the chimneys of Vulcan's forge!

Do you know the difference between magma and lava?

137. Magma is molten rock. Lava is magma that has gotten to the surface. Depending on the specific volcano and the magma under it, the lava may flow slowly out of the ground or explode violently.

138. Lava can get as hot as 1,200 degrees Celsius (2,200 degrees Fahrenheit)—hot enough to melt rocks and metals!

139. Volcanoes are grouped into three: shield volcanoes, stratovolcanoes, and cinder cones.

140. Shield volcanoes, like Mauna Loa, have gentle slopes and ooze lava slowly, while stratovolcanoes like Mt Fuji in Japan are steep and explosive. Cinder cones are small and made of volcanic ash and rocks.

141. Mauna Loa in Hawaii is the largest shield volcano in the world. It's so massive that it makes up half of the island of Hawaii.

142. Ojos del Salado is the world's tallest active volcano.

143. Supervolcanoes, such as Yellowstone Caldera, are capable of eruptions thousands of times larger than normal volcanoes.

Interactive Activity: Creating a Fun Volcano

Let's use baking soda and vinegar to create a fizzy eruption. This is a fun way to see how pressure builds up and is released during a volcanic eruption!

1. Add a spoonful of baking soda to a cup.
2. Slowly pour in vinegar to watch the baking soda bubble.
3. Keep pouring vinegar until the baking soda bubbles over the sides of the cup.

Sub-section 2.2: Seismic Waves and Earth's Vibrations

How do scientists detect and study earthquakes?

144. Seismographs that measure seismic waves! These seismic waves are vibrations from an earthquake that travel through the ground.

145. There are different types of seismic waves. P-waves zoom fast and squish things like a slinky. S-waves wiggle slowly from side to side and shake more. Surface waves cause the most shaking and can wreck buildings!

Can earthquakes be predicted?

146. Not really yet, but scientists use data from past quakes to improve early warning systems.

What should you do in an earthquake?

147. Drop to the ground, find cover, and hold on! Find a safe place under a sturdy table to protect yourself.

Interactive Activity: The Ripple Effect

Drop a small stone in a pool of water and watch the ripples spread out like seismic waves. This experiment highlights the way seismic waves spread out during an earthquake.

Sub-section 2.3: Resilience and Renewal

148. Volcanoes and earthquakes can cause damage to property and life, but they also reshape the land. Lava even cools into land.

149. In Iceland, crops like potatoes are grown in volcanic soil. This is because volcanic soil contains a lot of ash which is good for certain crops.

150. After the 1906 San Francisco earthquake, better and stronger buildings were rebuilt in the city.

151. Earthquakes in Japan created hot springs that are now enjoyed by the local community

152. Mount St. Helens erupted in 1980, but plants and animals have slowly returned. Scientists and engineers assisted the involved communities to prepare and recover.

Interactive Activity: Environmental Restoration Project

Try planting some crops on barren land. You can mix ash into the soil to boost its quality. Pretend that you are restoring an area damaged by a volcano.

Section 3: Global Scientist Spotlight – Geology Innovators

Let us meet some geology heroes!

Sub-section 3.1: Early Geology Pioneers

153. James Hutton (Scotland) is widely referred to as the father of geology. He was instrumental in cementing the idea that our history can be inferred from present-day rocks.

154. Alfred Wegener (Germany) proposed the idea of continental drift in 1912, suggesting that continents were once joined together.

155. Mary Anning (England) found dinosaur bones that showed Earth's past.

156. Marie Tharp (USA) created the first maps of the ocean floor, proving plates move! She also found underwater mountains.

157. Harry Hess (USA) helped discover seafloor spreading, confirming how continents shift over time.

158. J. Tuzo Wilson (Canada) helped develop the plate tectonic theory.

Interactive Activity: Making a Fossil

Make a fossil! Press a leaf or shell into clay and let it dry. Let's hope two centuries from now, a geologist would find that shell and learn about our generation from it.

Sub-section 3.2: Contemporary Earth Scientists

159. Today, geologists like Tanya Atwater and Marcia McNutt study plate tectonics, volcanoes, and earthquakes.

160. Katia and Maurice Krafft (France) were volcanologists who studied eruptions up close.

161. Toshitaka Katsura (Japan) researches deep Earth materials.

162. Inge Lehmann (Denmark) discovered Earth's inner core.

163. Charles Richter (USA) developed the Richter scale for measuring earthquakes.

164. Zhonghe Zhou (China) digs up rocks to learn Earth's history. He also described "Confuciusornis," an ancient bird.

Interactive Activity: Know A Geologist

Look up a modern geologist, like Kathryn Sullivan who was both an astronaut and an oceanographer. What did she discover about the Earth?

Sub-section 3.3: Inspiring Young Earth Explorers

Kids can become geologists too!

165. In 2014, three twelve-year-old sixth graders travelled to Spain to win a geology competition. Their project was to design quake-proof structures.

How can I become a geologist?

166. If you love rocks, fossils, and exploring the outdoors, you might want to become a geologist! You can start by joining a geology club, visiting natural history museums, or even participating in science fairs.

When is the next local science fair around you? Be there and learn more!

Chapter Takeaways

- Large tectonic plates actually create the surface of the Earth as we see it .
- As they move, tectonic plates cause earthquakes and volcanoes.
- Mountains are formed when plates collide and erosion shapes the landscape over time.
- Scientists use seismographs to study earthquakes and predict future disasters.
- Early and modern geologists have made incredible discoveries about Earth's processes.

Chapter 3: Oceanic Mysteries – Exploring the Deep Blue

Discover the ocean's depths by plunging into a realm of glowing creatures, towering underwater mountains, and ancient shipwrecks. What secrets lie beneath the waves?

Did you know?

"We've only explored approximately 20% of the worlds' oceans? That leaves over 80% still to explore. "

Section 1: Marine Biodiversity and Ecosystems

Earth's oceans burst with life, from tiny specks to massive whales. Let's make a splash!

Sub-section 1.1: Coral Reefs – Underwater Rainforests

167. Coral reefs are underwater cities full of fish and amazing colors. These coral reefs are built by tiny animals called coral polyps (or simply 'corals').

168. Corals team up with tiny algae called zooxanthellae for food and color. Zooxanthellae live inside them and make them bright.

169. While 25% of all sea creatures live in reefs, those reefs only make up 1% of the ocean!

Why are coral reefs called the ' rainforests of the Sea?'

170. Coral reefs host thousands of types of fish, plants, and other marine life. They're incredibly diverse, just like rainforests on land.

171. The Great Barrier Reef in Australia is so big you can see it from space. It is the largest in the world and stretches over 2,300 kilometers.

172. Reefs are awesome and serve very important functions. They are homes for fish, shield coasts from big waves, and even help produce oxygen!

173. Pollution and warm water can make these reefs sick or bleach them white

Interactive Task: Make Your Own Underwater Rainforest

Task : Draw a reef with fish, turtles, and corals—use your favorite colors and add your favorite aquatic animals.

Sub-section 1.2: Life in the Deep

The deeper you go, the stranger the creatures become!

174. Scientists estimate that millions of deep-sea species are yet to be discovered.

What is the midnight zone?

175. This is a region of the deep ocean where no sunlight reaches and animals rely on bioluminescence (glowing in the dark) or scavenging.

Why do some creatures rely on bioluminescence?

176. These creatures produce their own light and glow to find prey, scare enemies away, or chat with friends!

How do deep-sea creatures survive?

177. Some of Earth's weirdest and most intriguing creatures live in the deep ocean, like anglerfish, giant squids, and bioluminescent jellyfish.

178. Creatures that live in the deep sea have special adaptations like bioluminescence, slow metabolisms, and strong pressure-resistant bodies.

179. The angler-fish lures prey with a glowing "fishing pole" on its head.

180. The giant squid has eyes as big as soccer balls to see in the dark. Squids can grow in length up to 13 meters. That is most likely longer than your school bus.

Interactive Activity: Create a Bioluminescent Creature

Use glow-in-the-dark paint or stickers to design your own deep-sea animal. How do you think this creature will use its light to survive in the deep ocean?

Sub-section 1.3: Microscopic Marine Marvels

What are plankton and why are they important?

181. Plankton are tiny organisms that float in the ocean.

182. Planktons can be plants (phytoplankton) or animals (zooplankton).

183. Plankton are positioned at the bottom of the ocean food chain, and yet they produce over half of the oxygen we breathe!

184. Some plankton (like dinoflagellates) glow, making waves sparkle at night.

185. Phytoplankton use sunlight to make food through photosynthesis, just like plants on land.

186. Zooplankton eat phytoplankton and are then eaten by larger animals, like fish and whales.

187. Whales, seals, and fish love snacking on krill, a type of zooplankton.

Interactive Activity: DIY Experiments to Observe Marine Microbes

Observe some plankton. If you live near the ocean, collect a water sample and look at it under a microscope. If not, you can watch videos of plankton online. What do you see?

Section 2: Technologies of Ocean Exploration

Because the ocean is so deep, scientists need special tools to see what's down there!

Sub-section 2.1: Mapping the Seafloor

How do scientists map the seafloor?

188. Sonar (sound waves)! Scientists use these waves to map the seafloor. A ship sends sound waves down to the ocean floor, and the waves bounce back, creating a picture of the seafloor's shape.

189. Satellites also help map the ocean by measuring the height of the water's surface.

190. Some special satellites can also detect underwater mountains and trenches from space!

191. The Pacific Ocean's Mariana Trench is over 36,000 feet deep!

192. Within the Mariana Trench is the Challenger Deep, which is deeper than Mt Everest is tall.

193. Sonar waves were used to find the wreckage of the *Titanic* in 1985.

Interactive Activity: Simulate Seafloor Mapping

Task 1: Let's make a seafloor map! Fill a baking dish with water and sand. Use a spoon to create mountains and valleys in the sand, then use a ruler to "map" the seafloor by measuring the depth of the water.

Sub-section 2.2: Deep-Sea Submersibles and Robotics

194. Human beings cannot dive beyond a certain depth because of the crushing pressure in the oceans.

195. We use submersibles (small submarines) and robots to dive deep into the sea. They can go deeper and stay longer, allowing us to learn even more.

196. Submersibles like *Alvin* and robots like ROVs (Remotely Operated Vehicles) have discovered new species, explored shipwrecks, and even studied hydrothermal vents on the ocean floor.

Why do we need deep-sea exploration?

197. Many deep-sea species and ecosystems remain undiscovered, and some may hold clues to medical and scientific advancements.

What are ROVs?

198. Remotely Operated Vehicles (ROVs) are robotic submersibles controlled from the surface to explore the deep sea.

199. ROVs can film the deep sea for several months without needing to surface.

When was the first manned deep-sea dive?

200. In 1960, Jacques Piccard and Don Walsh went into the Mariana Trench in the *Trieste.*

201. In 2012, *The Deepsea Challenger,* piloted by Hollywood director, James Cameron, made it all the way to the bottom of the Mariana Trench.

Interactive Activity: Build Simple Underwater Models

Use a plastic bottle, straws, weights, and clay to create a model that can sink and float in water. Then, try your submersible in a pool. Did it sink beneath the surface? Good!

Sub-section 2.3: Global Initiatives in Marine Science

202. Countries around the world collaborate on ocean research through organizations like UNESCO and the United Nations.

203. Global initiatives like the Ocean Observing System and Census of Marine Life have helped scientists discover thousands of new species.

204. We use buoys and satellites to track fish, waves, and weather. Buoys can remain afloat for a long time and continue to send info about the sea!

How does ocean pollution affect the whole planet?

205. Trash, chemicals, and oil spills in one part of the ocean can spread and harm marine ecosystems everywhere.

206. Over 100 countries work together on ocean science and the data they collect helps to stop overfishing and pollution.

What are some current conservation efforts?

207. Organizations like the Ocean Cleanup Project work to remove plastic from the ocean, while marine protected areas help safeguard marine species.

What can you do to help?

208. Yes, you can help in your own little way. Plastic is very harmful to ocean life. You can try to use less plastic and join beach cleanups!

Interactive Activity: Take a Virtual Dive Tour and Explore Online Labs

Get online and search "Virtual Ocean Labs" for awesome sea tours that will give you an idea of just how wonderful the oceans are!

Section 3: Global Scientist Spotlight – Marine Pioneers

Ocean lovers from all over the world have explored the deep seas. Let's meet some of these legendary wave-makers!

Sub-section 3.1: Legendary Ocean Explorers

Long before modern submersibles, sailors and scientists were studying the ocean.

Early ocean explorers used primitive equipment and diving to study the ocean. Therefore, their findings were limited. Nevertheless, they discovered new species, explored coral reefs, and explained why looking after the ocean is so crucial.

209. The first oceanographers were Greek and Chinese people from cultures that lived in coastal areas.

210. Their first recorded dives into the ocean were as far back as 5000 B.C.

211. Polynesians, Vikings, and Chinese explorers navigated vast ocean distances using the stars and currents.

Have you heard of Matthew Maury?

212. Known as the "Father of Oceanography," he created some of the first ocean current maps. His "Wind and Current" chart of the North Atlantic was published in 1847.

213. Sir John Murray was a Canadian-born British oceanographer, marine biologist and limnologist often referred to as the Father of Modern Oceanography.

214. Thor Heyerdahl, a Norwegian, sailed a raft to prove that ocean travel was possible.

215. Jacques Cousteau jointly invented an underwater breathing apparatus, the Aqua-Lung, making scuba diving possible.

Interactive Activity: Meet an Early Ocean Explorer

Research an early ocean explorer, like William Beebe, who was one of the first to explore the deep sea. What did he discover? You can look at other early explorers, too.

Sub-section 3.2: Modern Marine Innovators

Who are some famous marine scientists, biologists and oceanographers today?

216. Asha de Vos, a Sri-Lankan, is at the forefront of blue whale research in the Indian Ocean.

217. Edith Widder was the first explorer to capture video of the giant squid in its home environment.

218. Sylvia Earle completed the deepest sea floor walk and has spent more than 7000 hours underwater.

219. Robert Ballard is popular for discovering the wreckage of the *Titanic* after several failed attempts by other explorers.

220. Exploring the oceans can be dangerous. On 18 June 2023, five people, including the CEO of OceanGate, operators of the *Titan* submersible, set out to explore the wreck of the *Titanic.*

221. One hour and 33 minutes into the dive, the mother ship lost communication with the *Titan*. Four days later, the wreckage of the *Titan* was found 500 meters from the *Titanic*. Sad!

Sub-section 3.3: Inspiring Future Oceanographers

If you like the oceans, nothing is stopping you from becoming a marine scientist, too.

222. Kids in the Maldives use snorkels to check reefs. They document and make reports of what they find on their expeditions.

223. Local junior ocean clubs around the world take young explorers like you on ocean exploration programs.

224. Children in Australia have been engaged in helping reduce the plastic content of the oceans.

Why not join an international marine science club now?

The ocean is waiting for you to explore it!

Chapter Takeaways

- The ocean is a vast world that we have not explored fully.
- Coral reefs are essential ecosystems that support marine life.
- Deep-sea creatures have amazing adaptations for survival.
- Scientists use sonar, satellites, and submersibles to explore the ocean.
- Marine researchers from around the world help protect our oceans.

Chapter 4: Microcosm Magic – The Hidden World of Life

"In every drop of water and speck of soil lies a universe of unseen life!"

Have you ever wondered about what lives in a single drop of water? It may look empty to the naked eye, but if you peered through a microscope, you'd see an entire world teeming with tiny creatures. These microscopic organisms shape life on Earth, influencing everything from our health to the environment.

Section 1: The Wonders of Microbiology

Sub-section 1.1: Cells – The Building Blocks of Life

225. Cells are the building blocks of all living things. Whether it's a towering tree, a buzzing bee, or even you, we are all made up of cells!

226. The primary cell types are prokaryotic cells (like bacteria) and eukaryotic cells (found in plants, animals, and fungi).

227. In higher animals like humans, cells make up tissue, tissues make up organs, organs make up a system, and the entire body contains several of these systems.

228. Nephrons (kidney cells) make up kidney tissue. The kidney itself is a part of the excretory system and the excretory system is just one of the systems in our bodies.

229. The human body is made up of about 37 trillion cells! That's more than the number of stars in the Milky Way galaxy!

How do cells function?

230. In the same way the human body has different parts and organs for different functions, each cell has special parts called organelles that perform different functions.

231. The nucleus stores genetic information, the mitochondria generate energy and the cell membrane controls what goes in and out of the cell.

232. There are other important organelles like ribosomes, golgi bodies and endoplasmic reticulum, too.

Are all cells the same size?

233. No! Some cells are so small they can only be seen with a microscope, while others, like an ostrich egg, are visible to the naked eye!

Do all cells have the same shape?

234. No! The shape and structure of each cell depends on its location and function.

235. Muscle cells are long and stretchy to help us move, while red blood cells are shaped like tiny donuts to carry oxygen through our bodies.

236. Nerve cells, or neurons, can be over a meter long in humans! They send electrical signals from your brain to the rest of your body, allowing you to move and feel sensations.

How do cells reproduce?

237. Most cells divide in a process called mitosis, creating identical copies to help organisms grow and heal.

238. Your skin cells replace themselves every few weeks—billions die and regrow daily.

239. Some cells, like bacteria, can divide every 20 minutes under the right conditions. That's why a single bacterium can multiply into millions in just a few hours!

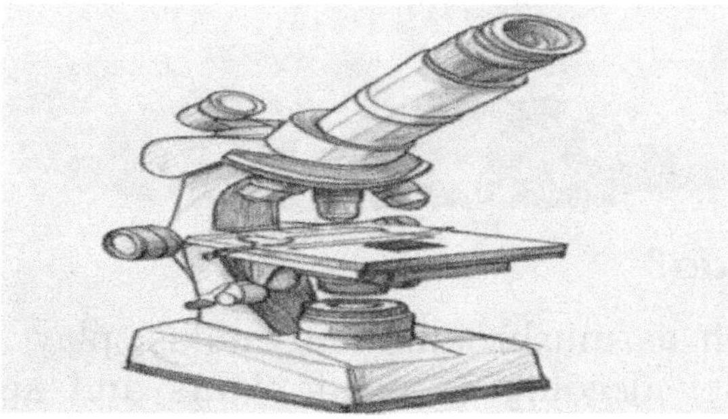

Interactive Activity: Microscope Activities to Explore Cell Biology

If you have access to a microscope, look at a drop of pond water or a slice of onion. Draw what you see and label the parts of the cells.

Sub-section 1.2: Microbes at Work

What are microbes?

240. Microbes, or microorganisms, are tiny living things that are too small to see with the naked eye.

241. Microbes include bacteria, viruses, fungi, and more. Regardless of their size, they have a significant impact on our world.

242. There are more microbes in your body than there are human cells. In fact, the human body is home to trillions of microbes, many of which help keep you healthy.

Are all microbes bad?

243. **NO!** Many microbes are actually helpful! For example, bacteria in your gut helps you digest food, and some bacteria are used to make yogurt and cheese.

244. Even viruses can be useful. Scientists can use them to deliver medicine to specific cells.

245. Some bacteria can 'eat' oil spills! These special bacteria break down the oil into harmless substances, helping to clean up the environment.

What do fungi do?

246. Fungi, such as mushrooms and molds, play a crucial role as decomposers. They decompose dead plants and animals, recycling nutrients back into the soil.

247. Some fungi are used to make medicines, like penicillin.

248. A fungus holds the title of the largest organism on Earth! Found in Oregon, there's a honey fungus that covers over 2,385 acres (about 1,600 football fields) and is over 2,400 years old!

How do microbes affect our health?

249. Some microbes can make us sick, like the flu virus or harmful bacteria. But many microbes are essential for our health.

250. The bacteria in our digestive system aid in food digestion and enhance our immune response.

251. Scientists are also studying how the microbes in our gut affect our mood and behavior. Research indicates that a balanced gut microbiome may aid in lowering stress and anxiety levels!

Interactive Activity: Growing Your Own Microbe

Let's grow some microbes! Take a cotton swab and swipe it on a surface, like a doorknob or your phone. Then, rub it on a piece of bread and seal it in a plastic bag. Leave it for a few days and observe what grows.

Sub-section 1.3: Genetics – The Code of Life

What is DNA?

252. DNA (deoxyribonucleic acid) is the molecule that conveys the instructions for constructing and sustaining an organism.

253. You share 99% of your DNA with everyone, but tiny differences make you unique.

254. Genetic variation means no two people (except identical twins) are exactly alike!

What are genes?

255. Genes are sections of DNA that contain the instructions for making specific proteins.

256. Proteins are the building blocks of your body and influence everything from your eye color to how your body combats infections.

257. We have about 20,000 to 25,000 genes, but some plants, like wheat, have over 100,000 genes.

Why do I look like my family?

258. You inherit genes from your parents and you will also pass them down to your children!

Can genes change?

259. Yes, genes can change through mutations.

260. Mutations are random changes in DNA that happen when cells divide or are exposed to things like radiation or chemicals.

261. Mutations are the reason we have so much diversity in life. For example, all dogs—from tiny Chihuahuas to giant Great Danes—come from the same ancestor, but mutations over thousands of years have created all the different breeds we see today.

What is genetic engineering?

262. This refers to the intentional act of trying to give an organism a new trait by altering its DNA.

263. Scientists utilize genetic engineering to develop crops that thrive in harsh conditions, such as drought or poor soil.

Interactive Activity: Extracting DNA from Fruit

Smash a banana, mix it with water and soap, then add alcohol. You'll see DNA strands appear!

Section 2: Biotechnology and Genetic Frontiers

Sub-section 2.1: Revolutionary Gene Editing

What is CRISPR?

264. CRISPR is a technology that enables scientists to edit genes with remarkable precision.

265. CRISPR acts like molecular scissors, excising unwanted DNA and inserting new instructions.

266. CRISPR was discovered in bacteria, which use it to fight off viruses. Scientists have adapted it to edit the DNA of plants, animals, and even humans.

How is CRISPR used in medicine?

267. CRISPR is utilized to treat genetic disorders such as sickle cell anemia by correcting the defective genes responsible for the disease. It's also being used to develop new cancer treatments.

268. In 2020, scientists used CRISPR to cure a patient of sickle cell anemia for the first time. Hopes are high!

Can CRISPR edit human embryos?

269. Yes, in theory, CRISPR can edit human embryos, but this is very controversial. It raises ethical questions about 'designer babies' and the long-term effects of editing human DNA.

270. Designer babies refers to babies who have been carefully selected and chosen for enhanced traits using advanced genetics techniques.

271. In 2018, a scientist in China claimed to have created the first genetically-edited babies.

What are the risks of CRISPR?

272. One risk of CRISPR is that it could make unintended changes to DNA, which could cause new problems.

Interactive Activity: An Ethical Debate

Let's debate! Should scientists be allowed to edit human embryos to prevent genetic diseases? What are the pros and cons? Discuss with a friend or family member.

Sub-section 2.2: From Lab to Life

How do scientists turn discoveries into real-world solutions?

273. When scientists make a new discovery, it takes some time before the discovery can be turned into something useful for everyone.

274. A newly-discovered drug might take several years of testing and tests before it is approved.

275. Creating new medications can take more than a decade and cost billions of dollars. Only a small fraction of experimental drugs ever make it to the market.

What is synthetic biology?

276. Synthetic biology allows scientists to design and build new biological systems or redesign existing ones.

277. Scientists have created synthetic bacteria that can glow in the dark! They did this by adding genes from a jellyfish. These 'bioluminescent' bacteria could one day be used to light up cities without electricity.

How is biotechnology used in agriculture?

278. Biotechnology can create crops that are more resistant to pests, diseases, and harsh weather.

279. Scientists have created genetically modified crops that can thrive in dry conditions, assisting farmers in regions with minimal rainfall.

280. Golden rice is a bioengineered variety enriched with vitamin A. It was created to combat vitamin A deficiency, a condition that can result in blindness in children.

281. In 2015, scientists created a genetically modified mosquito that could help fight malaria. The mosquito carries a gene that prevents it from spreading the disease.

Interactive Activity: Exploring Genetic Tools with Digital Labs

Imagine you could create a new plant or animal. What modified or new traits would it have? Create an illustration and compose a brief description of how it could benefit individuals or the environment.

Sub-section 2.3: The Future of Biological Science

Can synthetic biology fix the planet?

282. Maybe! It may solve important problems like pollution or allow us to grow food fast.

283. Scientists from all over the world are investing time, skills and ideas into synthetic and molecular biology. Already, scientists can create artificial/synthetic cells that can mimic normal cells.

284. In 2010, researchers developed the first synthetic cell, named Mycoplasma laboratorium. It was made by inserting artificial DNA into a bacterial cell, effectively creating a new form of life.

What are biofactories?

285. Biofactories are living organisms, like bacteria or yeast, that are engineered to produce useful substances.

286. Scientists have created bacteria that can produce insulin, an important medicine for people with diabetes.

287. Some biofactories are being used to try to produce spider silk, which is a material potentially stronger than steel.

288. Spider silk may eventually be used to make bulletproof vests or medical sutures.

289. Some scientists are also working on bringing back extinct species such as the woolly mammoth.

290. In the future, treatments may be tailored to a person's DNA, or we may even have the ability to cure genetic diseases before birth.

291. Research is underway to develop 'carbon-eating' bacteria that could absorb carbon dioxide from the atmosphere and help combat global warming.

Interactive Ability: Living in a Biotech-Powered Future

Let's imagine the future! What do you think the world will look like in 50 years if synthetic biology becomes common? Write a short story about a day in the life of someone living in a world with advanced biotechnology.

Section 3: Global Scientist Spotlight – Biological Innovators

From time immemorial, even before we had the tools to see them, curious minds have tried to see into the world of microbes.

Sub-section 3.1: Early Pioneers in Biology

Who laid the foundations for modern biology to thrive?

292. Louis Pasteur from France is often credited as the 'Father of Microbiology.' Pasteur proved clearly that microbes cause diseases and food decay.

293. Building on that, he introduced pasteurization, which is a tool we still use today for killing harmful microbes in milk and preserving food.

294. Pasteur's work allowed for the development of vaccines for rabies and anthrax.

295. The Dutch scientist, Antoine Van Leeuwenhoek, holds the honor of being the first to view bacteria through a microscope.

296. Gregor Mendel, an Austrian biologist and monk, provided a clear direction about genetics and inheritance of traits.

297. By studying the height of pea plants, he created Mendel's Law, which reshaped how other scientists view inheritance. He is often referred to as the 'Father of Genetics.'

298. The DNA double-helix (twisted ladder) shape was actually first discovered by Rosalind Frank but she was not fully recognized for her contributions during her lifetime.

You must have heard of Charles Darwin. What did he do?

299. Charles Darwin formulated the theory of evolution through natural selection. He explained that humans evolved as a consequence of our adaptation to the environment.

300. Darwin's book, "On the Origin of Species" is one of the most important and widely read books in scientific history.

Interactive Activity: On the Shoulders of an Ancient Giant

Which other early biologists do you know? What are they famous for? What challenges did they face?

Sub-section 3.2: Modern Leaders in Biotechnology

Modern scientists have continued to build on what the early pioneers achieved.

Do you remember CRISPR?

301. Well, Jennifer Doudna, an American biochemist, co-invented CRISPR, the gene scissors. Together with Emmanuelle Charpentier, a French microbiologist, she received the Nobel Prize in Chemistry in 2020.

302. Charpentier and Doudna became the first female duo to win a Nobel Prize in scientific fields.

303. Craig Venter is an American biologist who was at the forefront of the effort to sequence the human genome.

304. George Church is an American geneticist who is known for his work on synthetic biology and gene editing. Church was also one of the pioneers of the Human Genome Project.

305. Katalin Kariko has done a lot for vaccine technology by working on mRNA vaccines that teach our bodies to fight microbes better.

Interactive Activity: Designer Babies-Science Taken Too Far?

Take a stand on the debate about designer babies. Weigh the pros and cons, and write a report about what you think of them.

Sub-section 3.3: Inspiring the Next Generation

If you love reading and watching content about animals, plants, and nature, then you are already a biology star in the making. You can take the next step forward by joining a science club, participating in science fairs, or even volunteering at a local lab or nature center.

What are some cool biology careers?

306. There are many exciting careers in biology, like marine biologists (studying ocean life), geneticists (studying DNA), or microbiologists (studying microbes). You could also work in biotechnology, developing new medicines or crops.

Want to hear something even cooler?

307. Some biologists work in space agencies, studying how life can survive in space or on other planets. This field is called astrobiology. Super cool, right?

Do you want to meet some young biology champions?

308. Gitanjali Rao is a young inventor who created a device to detect lead in water.

309. In 2020, Gitanjali Rao became Time magazine's inaugural 'Kid of the Year' due to her groundbreaking contributions in science and technology.

310. Boyan Slat is a young environmentalist who developed a system to clean up plastic in the ocean.

Finally, why not start your own biology project today?

You could study the plants and animals in your backyard, or even try growing your own microbes in a petri dish. The world of biology is waiting for you to explore and there is absolutely nothing to stop you!

Chapter Takeaways

- Cells are the foundation of all life.
- Microbes help or bug us—they're everywhere!
- Your DNA is your unique code that makes you, you.
- DNA carries instructions for all living things.
- CRISPR is a very important tool for editing genes.

- Biotech is poised to continue to make life better by transforming medicine, food, and conservation.
- Scientists around the world continue to explore life's mysteries and you can become one of them.

Chapter 5: Forces Unleashed – The World of Physics

"From the pull of gravity to the mystery of quantum particles, physics explains the magic behind everyday life!"

Every technological marvel—from smartphones to space travel—relies on fundamental physics. How do invisible forces shape the world around you? What keeps you firmly on the ground on Earth? Why can astronauts in space float? Have you ever wondered how balls bounce or heavy planes fly?

Physics is the science of how things move, work, and even get weird. It is the study of motion, energy, and forces that shape the universe.

In this chapter, we'll explore these forces, energy, and mind-bending ideas, and meet brilliant physicists from around the world.

Section 1: Fundamentals of Motion and Energy

For you to understand physics better, let's start with how stuff moves and powers up. Jump in!

Sub-section 1.1: Newton's Laws in Action

Do you remember Sir Isaac Newton from our discussions about astronomy and gravity?

311. Sir Isaac Newton made three very important rules about motion that explain how everything moves.

312. Sir Newton's rules are known as the Newton's Law of Action and Reaction

What is Newton's First Law?

313. Also referred to as the Law of Inertia, this law states that an object will either stay at rest or continue moving in a straight line unless acted upon by an external force.

314. Newton's Second Law states that that force equals mass times acceleration (F=ma). This means that heavier objects need more force to move. That makes a lot of sense, right?

315. Newton's third law asserts that every action has an equal and opposite reaction.

316. Sir Isaac Newton came up with these laws in 1687 and they're still used today to design everything from cars to rockets.

317. Rockets work because of Newton's Third Law. The rocket pushes exhaust gases down and the gases push the rocket up into space!

What is inertia?

318. Inertia is how objects resist changes in their motion. For example, if you're in a car that suddenly stops your body keeps moving forward because of inertia.

319. Before an object can change its motion the external force that is causing the change must be stronger than the object's inertia. That is why you cannot push your mom's car by yourself.

320. The more mass (weight) an object has the more inertia it has. That's why it's harder to push a heavy box than a light one!

321. In French, "force" is still "force." Pronounce it: "fors!"

What is acceleration?

322. Acceleration refers to how quickly an object's speed or direction changes.

323. Deceleration is the opposite of acceleration. It is the rate at which an object's speed reduces.

324. To calculate acceleration, subtract the initial speed from the final speed, and divide by the time taken.

What land animal has the fastest acceleration?

325. The cheetah! In the animal kingdom, the cheetah possesses the fastest acceleration, reaching 60 miles per hour from a standstill in just seconds.

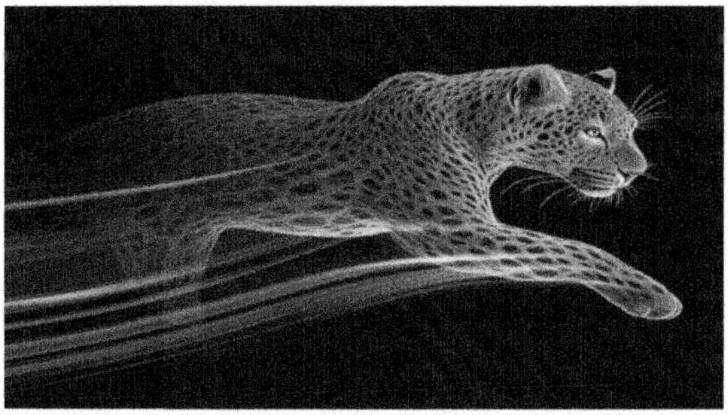

Interactive Activity: Testing the Laws of Motion

It is time to test Newton's Laws! Roll a ball across the floor and observe how it moves. What happens when it hits a wall? How does this demonstrate Newton's Laws? Which of the Laws does this demonstrate?

Sub-section 1.2: Energy in Transformation

What is energy?

326. Energy is the ability to get work done.

327. Energy can be kinetic energy (energy in motion) or potential energy (stored energy).

328. Energy also comes from different sources. Chemical energy is created as a product of chemical reaction, thermal energy is created by heat, and solar energy is created by the sun.

329. There is a very important law that guides energy. That is the Law of Conservation of Energy. It says that energy can't be created or destroyed but can only change forms.

Do you know what kinetic energy is?

330. Kinetic energy is the energy of motion.

331. A rolling ball has kinetic energy because it's moving. The faster it rolls, the more kinetic energy it has. A moving car also has kinetic energy.

Now, let's discuss potential energy.

332. Potential energy is stored energy. For example, a ball at the top of a hill has potential energy because it can roll down (but it's not currently rolling, which would be kinetic energy). The higher the hill, the more potential energy the ball has.

What is thermal energy?

333. Thermal energy is obtained from heat. It comes from the movement of tiny particles called atoms and molecules. The faster they move the hotter something feels.

334. The Sun generates a lot of thermal energy through nuclear fusion, where hydrogen atoms combine to form helium.

335. Nuclear fusion powers the Sun and gives us light and heat.

Why do we feel heat?

336. Heat energy transfers from warmer objects to cooler ones through conduction, convection, or radiation.

Interactive Activity: Energy Conversion

Rub your palms together fast until you feel some heat between your palms. What has just happened? What type of energy conversion occurred?

Kinetic energy was transformed into heat which is thermal energy. Did you get it? Thumbs up!

Sub-section 1.3: Gravity and Friction Uncovered

Gravity is not just the force that keeps us on our feet. It is much more than that.

What is gravity?

337. Gravity is the force that pulls objects (even planets) toward each other.

338. On Earth, gravity pulls everything toward the center of the planet, which is why things fall to the ground.

339. Gravity keeps the Moon moving around our planet and it also keeps the Earth in the Sun's orbit. Without gravity we would all float off into space!

340. There is a mathematical value for acceleration due to gravity on Earth. It is 9.8 meters per second squared! That is the rate at which gravity pulls everything towards the surface of the Earth.

341. On the moon, gravity is only 1/6th of Earth's. You'd jump higher than Micheal Jordan there! Basketball should be fun on the moon then!

Why do astronauts float in space?

342. They are in free-fall, moving around Earth at the same speed as their spacecraft.

Why don't things keep moving forever?

343. Inertia keeps them going, but friction slows them down.

344. Friction is the force that opposes motion between two surfaces.

345. Friction generates heat and causes wear and tear of surfaces. Rub your dry palms together slowly. Can you sense some friction as you rub your palms together? If you keep it up, you may even start to feel some heat.

346. Friction can be reduced through lubrication with a fluid. That is why engines need engine oil, for lubrication and to reduce wear and tear of the moving parts.

347. If you throw a ball gravity will pull it back down eventually, making it follow a curved path called a parabola.

What does friction do?

348. It grabs and slows things—like brakes on a bike!

349. Friction is essential for many things, such as walking, driving, and even writing with a pencil.

350. Without friction, we wouldn't be able to grip objects or stop moving!

351. Without friction, we wouldn't be able to walk upright. The friction between our feet and the ground keeps us from slipping.

352. Without gravity, there would be nothing stopping us from floating away into space.

353. Gravity and friction allow us to walk, run and jump the way we do.

354. Some animals, like geckos, use friction to climb walls. Their feet have tiny hairs that create a strong grip, allowing them to stick to almost any surface.

Interactive Activity: The Effect of Lubrication on Friction

Rub your dry palms together. What did you notice?

Now, pour some water on your palms. Rub them together again. What difference did you notice?

Did your palms slide over each other more easily? That's because water serves as a lubricant between both of your palms. Now, you know why cars need lubricants.

Section 2: Quantum Realms and Relativity

Physics gets wild with tiny bits and big space-time ideas. Let's explore!

Sub-section 2.1: Entering the Quantum World

In the quantum world, tiny things act strange—like particles and waves at once!

355. The term "quantum" originates from a Latin word that means "how much."

What is quantum physics?

356. Everything—your house, your dog, even you—is made of tiny particles that include electrons, protons, and neutrons. Quantum physics is all about how these bits behave.

357. Quantum physics is the study of the smallest particles in the universe, like atoms and subatomic particles. It explains how these particles behave in ways that are very different from the everyday world.

What are quantum particles?

358. A quantum particle is the smallest piece of something, like an electron (a tiny piece of an atom).

359. Atoms, the smallest unit of a substance, are made up of a central core called the nucleus and negatively-charged electrons distributed in orbitals.

360. The nucleus consists of positively-charged protons and neutral neutrons.

361. Electrons zip around the center of atoms so fast they're like a blurry cloud instead of a dot. You won't catch them standing still!

362. As they gain or lose energy, electrons change their orbitals.

363. Quantum particles are the building blocks of matter. They include electrons, protons, and neutrons, as well as even smaller particles like quarks and photons.

What are quarks?

364. Protons and neutrons consist of these smaller particles called quarks. Quarks are so small that we have never seen them but we know they are there.

365. In the quantum world, particles can exist in two places at once, or even teleport from one place to another.

What is quantum entanglement?

366. Imagine that you have two magic coins. If you flip one and it lands on heads, the other coin will instantly land on tails, no matter how far apart they are. This is called entanglement, and it's a real phenomenon in quantum physics!

367. Particles can also sneak through walls like ghosts! It's called quantum tunneling, and it's how the sun's energy gets out to warm us up.

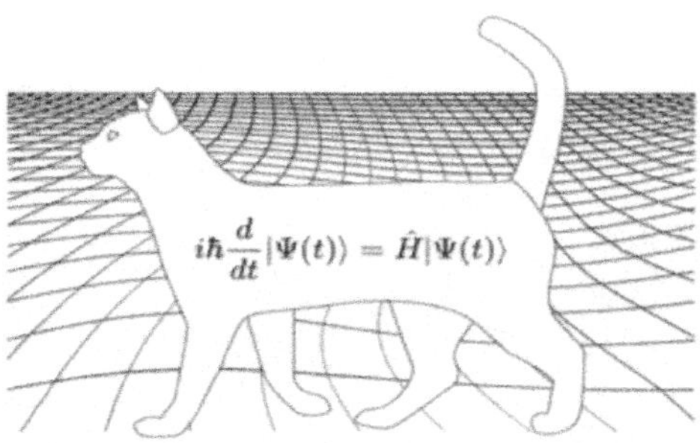

Have you heard of Schrondiger's cat?

368. Schrodinger's cat is not a real cat. It is a famous thought experiment that asks you to imagine a cat in a closed box with a mechanism that can kill it. Until you look inside that box, the cat is both dead and alive. Yet, the moment you look inside the box, it can only be in one of the two states. It explains quantum superposition.

369. Schrondiger's Cat was first used as an analogy by Erwin Schrondiger in 1935 while he was in a discussion with Albert Einstein.

What is the wave-particle duality?

370. Sometimes, light and electrons act like particles; other times, they act like waves.

371. Light can act like a wave (like ripples in water) or a particle (like tiny bullets of energy called photons.

372. Light is made of tiny packets called photons. Every time you see a rainbow, you're seeing photons at work!

373. Photons are particles of light. They have no mass, but they carry energy and can travel at the speed of light.

What is the uncertainty principle?

374. The uncertainty principle says that you can't know both the position and the speed of a particle at the same time. The more you know about one, the less you know about the other. It's like trying to guess where a bumblebee or buzzing fly will go next!

375. The uncertainty principle was discovered by Werner Heisenberg in 1927. It's one of the most important ideas in quantum physics.

376. Another explanation of the uncertainty principle is that electrons zip around atoms but don't have exact positions.

377. The principle says if you figure out a particle's speed really well its position gets fuzzy, and vice versa. It's a trade-off in the quantum world.

Have you heard of quantum computers?

378. A quantum computer is a new type of computer that uses quantum particles to perform calculations.

379. Quantum computers are capable of solving problems significantly more quickly than traditional computers. This could revolutionize fields like medicine and cryptography.

380. Quantum computers are still in the early stages of development, but companies like Google and IBM are already building prototypes. They could change the world in the next few decades. Or sooner!

Why does quantum physics matter?

381. It helps to power phones, MRIs, computers, and even some futuristic teleportation experiments!

382. LEDs (those bright lights in your TV or flashlight) work because of quantum physics. Electrons jump around and release light in a special way.

383. Your phone's microchip works using quantum physics!

384. Lasers (like the ones in DVD players or laser pointers) work because of quantum physics. They use photons, the particles of light, to create a focused beam.

385. Nuclear fusion in the sun only happens because of quantum particles interacting at the sun's core.

386. Astronomers use the knowledge of quantum physics to determine the chemical composition and age of distant stars.

387. Quantum physics tells us how stars shine, how the sun makes energy, and even how the tiniest pieces of space stick together.

Interactive Activity: Simulations to Visualize Quantum Phenomena.

Let's simulate quantum particles! Get a flashlight and a piece of paper. Create small holes in the paper to create a particle beam. Shine the light through the holes and observe how it behaves. Do you think light is a wave now? How do your observations show the wave-particle duality of light?

Sub-section 2.2: The Mysteries of Relativity

What is relativity?

388. Relativity as a theory was developed by Albert Einstein to explain how time, space, and gravity work.

389. Special relativity deals with objects moving at constant speeds.

390. General relativity deals with gravity and acceleration.

391. The theory of general relativity was first published back in 1915, but the theory of special relativity was published ten years before that. These theories completely changed our understanding of the universe.

How does relativity affect our GPS?

392. GPS satellites have to account for both special and general relativity to give accurate locations.

393. Einstein's theories are so precise that GPS systems have to adjust for time differences of just a few billionths of a second to work correctly.

394. It is a proven fact that time expands or shrinks in cases of extreme speed or strong gravity, a concept known as time dilation.

395. Time dilation has been proven by experiments with atomic clocks. A clock on a fast-moving airplane ticks slightly slower than a clock on the ground.

396. If you put a clock on a tall mountain and a similar clock on the beach, the clock on top of the mountain will be faster because there is less gravity up there.

What is space-time?

397. Space-time is the idea that space and time are not separate but are connected in a four-dimensional fabric.

398. Space-time is like a big, flexible sheet where space and time work together. Heavy objects, like the sun, create dents in this sheet, and that's how gravity pulls things toward them.

399. Space-time has four dimensions: up-down, left-right, forward-backward, and time. It's like a 4D grid where everything in the universe has a place and a time.

400. Near a black hole, time almost stops. If you watched someone there, they'd look like they're moving in super slow motion!

401. Astronauts in space age just a tiny bit slower than people on Earth because they're speeding around the planet. They're like mini time travelers!

402. If one twin blasts off in a speedy spaceship and the other stays home, the space twin comes back younger! It's like time travel but with real science.

403. When huge things in space crash or explode they make wiggles in space-time called gravitational waves.

How does gravity shape space-time?

404. Gravity can actually bend space-time. The sun causes curves in space-time and that is why planets orbit around it.

405. When light goes past something heavy, like a star, light bends.

406. Black holes have so much gravity that even light cannot escape them.

407. Some scientists think there could be tunnels in space-time called wormholes. They think that they might be secret passages to zip across the universe super fast!

408. Nothing can travel faster than light—it's the fastest thing in the universe. According to relativity, if you could travel at the speed of light, time would stop for you!

Why can't we travel faster than light?

409. According to relativity, the faster you go, the heavier you get. If you tried to reach the speed of light, you'd need infinite energy, which is impossible!

410. According to relativity, if you could travel faster than light or get close to a black hole, you might be able to travel through time. But no one has figured out how to do it yet.

411. Light travels so fast that, from its perspective, time doesn't pass. A photon of light could cross the universe without "feeling" any time at all!

412. Einstein's equation, $E = mc^2$, tells us that energy (E) and mass (m) are related.

413. Relativity and quantum physics don't always agree. Relativity explains big things like stars and galaxies, while quantum physics explains tiny things like atoms.

414. Black holes are where relativity and quantum physics meet! Black holes are so weird that they challenge both relativity and quantum physics.

Interactive Activity: Space-Time Demonstration

Use a large sheet of fabric and a heavy ball to simulate how gravity bends space-time. Place the ball in the center of the fabric and observe how it creates a gravity well. Roll smaller balls around the edge to see how they orbit the well caused by the heavy ball.

Sub-section 2.3: Particle Physics in Focus

Particle physics looks at tiny particles that make up everything in the universe, smaller than atoms.

What is the Standard Model?

415. It is a theory that explains how the basic building blocks of matter (like quarks and electrons) interact through forces like electromagnetism and both strong and weak nuclear forces.

416. There are 4 force-carrying particles: photons are associated with electromagnetism, gluons mediate the strong force, W and Z bosons are responsible for the weak force, and the Higgs boson provides mass.

417. The Standard Model has been incredibly successful, but it doesn't explain everything—like gravity or dark matter.

Do you remember quarks?

418. Yes! Quarks are tiny particles that combine to form protons and neutrons in atoms.

419. Quarks come in six different types which include: up, down, charm, strange, top, and bottom.

420. Protons and neutrons are made of up and down quarks.

421. Protons are made of quarks—two "up" quarks and one "down" quark—glued together by particles called gluons.

422. Neutrons are made up of one "up" quark and two "down" quarks

423. Quarks are never found alone—they're always bound together in groups of two or three. This is called quark confinement.

424. The name "quark" came from a book —James Joyce's *Finnegans Wake.*

425. Murray Gell-Mann proposed the quark theory in 1964.

What is antimatter?

426. It is the opposite of normal matter. If it touches regular matter, they destroy each other in a burst of energy.

427. For every particle of matter, there is a corresponding particle of antimatter. But almost all antimatter disappeared after the Big Bang.

428. The existence of antimatter was first predicted by Paul Dirac in 1928 and discovered with the positron in 1932.

What is the Higgs boson?

429. The Higgs boson, also called the 'God particle,' was discovered in 2012, confirming how particles get their mass!

430. The Higgs boson is sometimes called the 'God particle' because it's so important to our understanding of mass. Without it, particles wouldn't have mass, and the universe as we know it wouldn't exist!

431. The Higgs boson gives other particles mass. It is like cosmic glue that holds everything together. It was discovered at the Large Hadron Collider (LHC) in Switzerland.

432. The discovery of the Higgs Boson fulfilled a prediction made almost 50 years earlier. The Brout-Englert-Higgs mechanism had predicted the existence of a fundamental particle with such properties.

433. The Higgs Boson is heavy and has a mass that is 125 times that of a proton. It also decays fairly quickly

How do scientists study particles?

434. Scientists use giant accelerators like the Large Hadron Collider to smash atoms together. The LHC is the world's largest particle accelerator.

435. The first particle accelerator was built in 1931 by Ernest Lawrence and it was called a cyclotron.

436. Particle accelerators can either be linear (straight line) accelerators or circular like the LHC.

437. The Large Hadron Collider smashes particles together at nearly the speed of light to study the fundamental building blocks of the universe.

438. The LHC is a 27-kilometer (17-mile) ring buried underground near Geneva, Switzerland. It's so big that it crosses the border between Switzerland and France!

439. Building the LHC was expensive. It involved 10,000 scientists from over 100 countries and cost $ 10 billion.

440. The Higgs boson adds mass—like magic dust!

441. Particle physics is important in medicine. Antimatter is used in hospitals during PET scans to see inside the body.

442. Tim Berners-Lee developed the World Wide Web at CERN, home to the LHC, to facilitate data sharing among scientists.

443. Small particle accelerators are used in TVs, X-ray machines, and even to sterilize food.

444. In Korean, 'physics' is 'mulli-hak' and spelt as '물리학.' Say it: mool-lee-hak! Cool stuff, right?

Interactive Activity : Virtual Tours of Particle Accelerators

There are many virtual LHC tours online. Search "LHC Virtual Tour" online to see what the real thing looks like. You will have a great time and lots of fun!

Section 3: Global Scientist Spotlight – Physics Visionaries

Sub-section 3.1: Classical Innovators

445. The study of physics began with observations of our physical world.

446. Archimedes was one of the earliest physicists. He discovered the principles of flotation one day as he lay in a bathtub.

447. Archimedes rushed through the streets of Greece from the bathtub shouting "Eureka! Eureka!" "Eureka" means "I found it."

448. Archimedes lived in Greece between 287–212 BCE and also invented pulleys and levers.

449. Ibn al-Haytham from Iraq advanced the field of optics with his work on light and vision. His book, *Book of Optics, provided* valuable information for the field of modern optics to build upon.

450. Ibn al-Haytham is famous for pretending to be mad to avoid a grumpy ruler. He also wrote 200 books in secret.

451. Shen Kuo was a Chinese scientist and statesman often credited with inventing the magnetic needle compass. His work on magnetism and fossils set the tone for this work more than 1,200 years ago.

452. Bhaskara, an Indian mathematician who lived between 1114-1185, wrote the *Siddhanta Shiromani,* which greatly influenced early thoughts about gravity and light reflection.

Who was Galileo Galilei?

453. Galileo Galilei improved the telescope, discovered the moons of Jupiter, and supported the idea that the Earth orbits the Sun.

Why was Galileo put on trial?

454. For science! Galileo was put on trial by the Catholic Church for saying that the Earth orbits the Sun. He was forced to recant his beliefs, but today we know he was right.

Who was Isaac Newton?

455. Isaac Newton was an English scientist who discovered the laws of motion and gravity. He also invented calculus and made groundbreaking discoveries in optics and mathematics.

456. Newton's discovery of gravity is often attributed to an apple falling from a tree. He realized that the same force that made the apple fall also kept the Moon in orbit around the Earth.

Who wrote the three laws of motion?

457. Yes! You got it right. Sir Newton did!

458. In the 17th century, Christiaan Huygens from the Netherlands made contributions to the field of optics and the wave theory of light. He also explained centrifugal force.

459. James Clerk Maxwell, a Scottish physicist, is celebrated for unifying electricity, magnetism, and light into a theory called electromagnetism.

460. Maxwell's work with electromagnetism laid the foundation for modern technologies like radio, television, and Wi-Fi.

461. Michael Faraday, an English chemist and physicist is often credited as the 'Father of Electricity' for his contributions.

462. Faraday was a notable figure in the development of the fields of electrochemistry, electromagnetism, and electrolysis.

463. His work led to the eventual invention and development of critical things like the electric motor, electric transformer, and electric generator.

Interactive Ability: Meet a Classical Physicist!

You know the drill. This time, I want you to choose one of the classical physicists above. Find out facts about them that we have not covered. What is the most interesting fact you found?

Sub-section 3.2: Modern Physics Trailblazers

The early 20th century was a really important period in physics. It gave birth to the rise of modern physics and consolidated the work of early physicists.

464. By now, you are familiar with Albert Einstein. His work on relativity was very important for the advancement of physics.

465. Niels Bohr from Denmark contributed a lot to our knowledge of atomic structure and quantum theory.

466. Einstein and Bohr had a series of public disagreements about quantum mechanics and their understanding of it.

467. In 1930, C.V. Raman received the Nobel Prize in Physics for discovering the Raman effect. He explained the inelastic scattering of photons by matter.

468. The Raman effect also explains why the oceans appear to be blue during the day.

469. From Austria, Erwin Schrödinger wrote the Schrödinger equation that described the behavior of particles.

470. Werner Heisenberg, a German, became famous for writing the uncertainty principle.

471. Marie Curie was a Polish-French physicist and chemist who discovered radioactivity. Radioactivity is now a key part of curing cancer and many industrial processes.

472. Curie became the first female Nobel Prize laureate and remains the only individual honored with Nobel Prizes in both physics and chemistry.

473. Unfortunately, Marie Curie was eventually killed by radioactive poisoning. At the time, people did not know that radioactivity was dangerous.

474. Her notebooks are still so radioactive that they're kept in lead-lined boxes. Lead blocks radioactivity.

475. In Pakistan, Abdus Salam played a pivotal role in the development of the Standard Model theory and won a Nobel Prize in 1979.

476. Global collaboration has always been evident in the physics world. Hideki Yukawa(湯川秀樹) of Japan won a Nobel Prize for predicting the *pi meson*. Chen Ning Yang from China worked extensively on particle physics.

477. Homi Bhabha, from India, was a forerunner of nuclear physics and studied cosmic rays.

478. Vera Rubins found it hard to persuade colleges to teach her astronomy and physics because she was a woman. She persisted and eventually discovered dark matter by studying spinning galaxies.

479. Richard Feynman was a famous American theoretical physicist who contributed the Parton model to the field of particle physics and was also responsible for the Feynman diagrams for subatomic particles.

480. Katherine Johnson was a black NASA scientist that calculated the Apollo Missions ***by hand.*** She broke big barriers as a black woman in tech while facing discrimination.

481. The Hollywood movie "Hidden Figures (2016)" starring Taraji Henson was based on the life of Katherine Johnson.

482. You now know Stephen Hawking as an important physicist but did you know about his discoveries of important facts about black holes and the origin of the universe?

483. Hawkings had a rare disease called ALS which left him paralyzed, but he continued to work and communicate using a speech-generating device.

What does that teach you?

484. We have no limits as humans!

Have you heard of Kip Thorne?

485. Kip Thorne is an American physicist who won the Nobel Prize for his work on gravitational waves.

486. Kip Thorne also helped make the Hollywood blockbuster movie "Interstellar" scientifically accurate.

487. Gravitational waves are ripples in space-time created by massive objects, like colliding black holes.

488. Gravitational waves were first detected in 2015, confirming a prediction made by Einstein 100 years earlier.

489. Fabiola Gianotti is an Italian physicist who was the first woman to lead CERN, the organization that runs the Large Hadron Collider.

490. Gianotti is not only a brilliant scientist but also a talented musician. She plays the piano and has even performed with orchestras! ***Multi-talented!***

Have you heard of string theory?

491. Michio Kaku is an American physicist and communicator who is known for his work on string theory and his popular science books and TV shows. String theory proposes that the universe consists of tiny, vibrating strings.

Interactive Activity: Meet Tesla

Did you know that Tesla cars were named after a Serbian-American engineer and scientist, Nikolai Tesla?

It is time for you to research and learn about Tesla. What were his most famous contributions? Who were his peers and competitors?

Sub-section 3.3: Lighting the Way for Future Physicists

How can I become a physicist?

492. If you love solving puzzles and asking big questions about the universe, you might want to become a physicist!

493. You can start by studying math and science in school, participating in science fairs, or even doing your own experiments at home.

I am bad with calculations. Can I become a physicist?

494. Many well-known physicists did not start off on the right foot. Albert Einstein was bad at mathematics as a kid, but he overcame his limitations to become perhaps the most famous scientist ever.

What does that teach you?

495. You can become whatever you want to be.

496. The most important thing you need right now is curiosity. Many famous physicists started out as just curious kids who wanted to know more about the world around them.

497. Anyone can be a physicist. From musicians to philosophers and Hollywood stars, physics has seen all kinds of people from all over the world. Physics needs everyone, including you!

What are some cool physics careers?

498. There are many exciting careers in physics, like astrophysics (studying stars and galaxies), quantum physics (studying tiny particles), or engineering (designing new technologies). You could even work in space exploration or renewable energy.

499. Some physicists work in video game design, using physics to create realistic movements and interactions in games. Physics is everywhere!

Are there young physicists that are making a difference?

500. Sabrina Gonzalez Pasterski is a young physicist who has been called the 'next Einstein' for her work on quantum gravity.

501. Pasterski started building her own airplane at age 14 and flew it solo in the US at age 16. She's now a leading researcher in theoretical physics.

502. In 2024, an 11-year-old boy from Shaoxing, China made headlines for building and launching his own rocket. To make the feat a success he wrote 600 lines of code for the rocket's control system. His family proudly supports him.

503. In 2017, as a 14-year-old, Eleanor Sigres from Virginia won a $25,000 prize at an engineering competition for a project that sought to improve cold gas nozzles in spacecraft.

How can I get involved in physics research now?

504. You can get involved in physics research by participating in science fairs, joining a physics club, or even working on your own experiments at home.

Interactive Activity: Join a STEM Club

STEM clubs are awesome for meeting like-minded individuals. You will also learn a lot of new stuff from the club and you can participate in competitions and webinars through the club. The best part is that you can find some of these clubs online. What are you waiting for? Search "Kids STEM" online!

Chapter Takeaways

- Newton's laws explain how objects move and interact with forces.
- Energy comes in many forms, like kinetic, potential, and thermal energy, and it can transform from one type to another.
- Gravity pulls everything toward Earth, while friction slows things down.
- Quantum physics and relativity reveal the strange and fascinating behavior of the universe on the smallest and largest scales.
- Theories of relativity explain space, time, gravity, and the relationship among all three.
- Early and modern physicists have made incredible discoveries that have changed the world.

You can become a physicist too—just follow your curiosity and explore the forces that shape the universe.

Chapter 6: Everyday STEM Adventures – Bringing Science Home

Did you know that you can turn your kitchen into a science lab, your backyard into a physics playground, and your art supplies into tools for discovery?

Let's transform your daily life into a continuous STEM adventure!

Section 1: Hands-On Experiments at Home

Sub-section 1.1: Kitchen Science

What occurs when you blend baking soda and vinegar?

505. Mixing baking soda with vinegar triggers a reaction that produces gas, leading to bubbles and fizz! This represents a straightforward chemical reaction.

506. This reaction is used in volcanoes for science fairs, but it's also how some fire extinguishers work!

507. The secret behind this reaction is that acids (like vinegar) and bases (like baking soda) team up to create something new—gas!

508. Carbon dioxide is the same gas that makes soda fizzy and the gas we breathe out!

509. Carbon dioxide is different from Carbon monoxide, CO.

510. CO is a toxic, odorless and colorless gas produced from the combustion that takes place in engines like car engines.

Can you make a rainbow in a glass?

511. Yes! By layering liquids of reducing densities, like honey, dish soap, water, and oil, you can create a colorful density tower. Try that today!

512. Density is how tightly packed the molecules in a substance are. Honey is denser than water, so it sinks to the bottom.

How does yeast make bread rise?

513. Yeast is actually a tiny fungus that eats sugar and releases carbon dioxide gas. CO_2 makes the dough rise and become fluffy.

514. Yeast has been used in baking for over 5,000 years. Ancient Egyptians were one of the first people to use it.

515. It is possible to prepare ice cream without needing a freezer. By mixing salt with ice, you can lower the temperature enough to freeze cream and sugar into ice cream. The salt makes the ice melt faster, absorbing heat from the cream.

516. This process used to make ice cream is called freezing point depression, and this is the reason salt is applied to melt ice on roads in winter, particularly in countries like Canada.

517. If you heat some milk in a microwave, add vinegar, and then use a strainer to remove the clumps that form, you will get milk that acts like plastic and can be folded into different shapes.

518. Milk acts this way because it contains a protein known as casein. Vinegar changes the pH of milk and causes it to curdle. The formed curds can be molded almost as if they were plastic.

You can also make eggs float and sink alternately!

519. If you place an egg in water, it will usually sink. However, if you add enough salt into the water, the egg will then float.

520. The egg sinks initially because the water is not dense enough to support its weight. Salt increases the water's density and makes the egg float.

Here is another experiment for you!

521. If you cut an apple into pieces and allow it to stay on a plate for some time, the pieces will become brown and appear stained. However, if you drop some lemon juice on the pieces, they will stay fresh and not get brown.

522. Apples become brown due to oxidation after they are exposed to oxygen in the air. Lemon juice prevents oxidation because of the citric acid it contains.

Do you want foam balls to pop out of your mouth?

523. Brush your teeth with a toothpaste that has baking soda as one of its ingredients. Do not spit out the toothpaste or rinse your mouth yet. Take a sip from a carbonated drink. Foam will begin to rise in your mouth and you can just watch it dribble out of your mouth.

524. The secret of this is that baking soda and phosphoric acid (from the carbonated drink) mix to cause the same type of chemical reaction in the vinegar experiment above. It is a base and acid reacting to create carbon dioxide gas yet again.

Like candy?

525. You can grow your own candy. To do this, dissolve sugar in hot water and then dip a string in the glass of sugar water. Let everything cool and you should see sugar crystals on the string like tiny rocks. If you add some coloring from the beginning, you will get a colorful candy.

How does heat change food?

526. Cooking transforms raw ingredients through processes like caramelization and coagulation. That is why food can taste very different after cooking.

527. Mix cornstarch and water to make a non-Newtonian fluid. Is the mixture a solid or a liquid?

Finally, let's make you a little spy scientist!

528. You can write secret invisible messages with lemon juice on paper. When you heat the paper, the message will become clear and obvious because heat will turn the lemon juice brown.

Interactive Activity: Make Your Own Ice Cream

In a small bag, mix together 1 cup of milk, 1 tablespoon of sugar, and 1/2 teaspoon of vanilla. Next, place this bag inside a larger one containing ice and 1/2 cup of salt. Shake for 5 minutes, and enjoy your homemade ice cream. Yummy!

Sub-section 1.2: Backyard Physics

How does a swing work?

529. A swing is a pendulum, which moves back and forth due to gravity and momentum.

530. On a swing, the higher you go the more potential energy you have, which turns into kinetic energy as you swing down.

531. The longest pendulum in the world is the Foucault Pendulum at the Pantheon in Paris. It proves the Earth rotates.

Can you make a parachute from a plastic bag?

532. Yes! Cut a square from a plastic bag, tie strings to the corners, and attach a small toy. When you drop it, the parachute slows the fall by catching air resistance.

533. Parachutes were first used in the 18th century, but the great Leonardo da Vinci sketched designs for them back in the 15th century.

534. The bounciest ball ever made is called a 'superball.' It can bounce over 10 feet high!

535. The superball was invented by Norman Stingley in the 1960s and made of Zectron.

536. The superball was the inspiration for the 'Super Bowl' name. The Super Bowl is among the largest sporting events in the world and has taken place since 1966.

How can you make a rainbow at home?

537. On a sunny day, spray water from a hose into the air. The sunlight will refract (bend) through the water droplets, creating a rainbow.

538. Rainbows are always circular, but we usually only see half of them because the ground blocks the rest.

Do heavier things fall faster to the ground?

539. No! Gravity pulls everything at the same speed, but air slows lighter stuff like feathers down.

540. Air resistance is the air pushing back—like a parachute slowing a fall. It is almost like friction that occurs in the air.

541. Astronauts on the Moon dropped a feather and a hammer, both hitting the ground simultaneously—no air resistance there!

Let us prove that Earth rotates!

542. By building a sundial! Stick a pencil in the ground and mark the position of its shadow every hour. The shadow moves as the sun does, proving that the Earth's rotation tells time!

Interactive Activity: Things Fall

Drop a heavy book and a feather from the same height. Do they fall at the same rate? Which one fell to the ground first? How can you explain the difference in their fall? Think gravity and air resistance!

Sub-section 1.3: The Art of Science

Science and art mix like paint colors!

Can you paint with science?

543. Yes! Mix baking soda with water to make paint, then use vinegar to create fizzy, colorful reactions on your paper.

544. This is called chemical art, and it's a fun way to blend creativity and science.

How do kaleidoscopes work?

545. Kaleidoscopes use mirrors to reflect light and create symmetrical patterns. When you turn the tube, the beads or pieces inside move, creating new designs.

546. The term 'kaleidoscope' originates from Greek words that translate to 'beautiful form to see.'

Can you make music with science?

547. Yes! Get some glass cups and fill them with different quantities of water. Then, tap them with a spoon. The vibrations create different pitches, turning your glasses into a musical instrument.

548. This is how glass harps work. Benjamin Franklin even invented a version called the 'armonica' in 1761!

What is tie-dye science?

549. Tie-dye uses chemical dyes that bond with fabric fibers. The patterns are created by folding and tying the fabric, which keeps the dye from reaching certain areas.

550. Tie-dye emerged as a symbol of peace and creativity in the 1960s and is particularly popular in Africa.

Why do bubbles create different shapes?

551. Surface tension and air pressure affect their structure differently.

552. Music is physics! When you pluck a rubber band, it vibrates to make sound. Stretch it tighter for a higher pitch!

553. You can mix glow paint with slime to make it shine. The paint absorbs light and re-emits it. That's an example of phosphorescence!

554. Leonardo da Vinci excelled as both a scientist and an artist. He studied anatomy to paint more realistically.

555. The golden ratio, found in many works of art, also appears in nature, like in flower petals and snail shells.

556. Artists use perspective to make their paintings look 3D, similar to how our eyes see depth. 3D paintings look very real.

557. Some artists use scientific techniques, like understanding light and shadow, to create realistic or abstract art.

Interactive Activity: Colorful Chromatography

Draw with markers on a coffee filter, then drip water on it. Colors spread and split. That's similar to how scientists separate mixtures using chromatographic techniques.

Section 2: Multilingual and Multicultural STEM

Sub-section 2.1: Celebrating Global Diversity in Science

How do different cultures contribute to science?

558. Every culture has unique ways of understanding the world. For example, Indigenous Australians used fire to manage forests and ancient Chinese astronomers mapped the stars.

559. The Mayans invented the concept of zero, which is essential for modern math and computers.

560. The Chinese invented papermaking, revolutionizing communication.

What is an astrolabe?

561. Ancient Islamic scientists developed this tool to study the stars.

Why do different cultures have unique counting systems?

562. Number systems evolved based on trade, navigation, and daily needs.

What is ethnobotany?

563. Ethnobotany is the study of how different cultures use plants for medicine, food, and tools. For example, Native Americans used willow bark as a pain reliever, which inspired aspirin.

564. West Africans have a rich ethnobotanical history with trees like the Neem tree used for a variety of ailments.

565. Over 25% of modern medicines come from plants used in traditional healing practices.

How do languages shape science?

566. Languages help us describe and share scientific ideas. For example, the Inuit have many words for snow, which helps them understand its different properties.

567. The periodic table is the same everywhere. Oxygen gas is represented as 'O_2' whether you speak French or Japanese. Science connects us!

568. 2+2=4 in English, Spanish, or Swahili. A circle always contains 360° no matter where you stand on the planet. Math is the global language of science!

569. The term 'algorithm' derives from the name of a 9th-century Persian mathematician, Al-Khwarizmi.

570. Arabic numerals, which we use today, were introduced from the Middle East to Europe.

571. Translating scientific books has helped spread knowledge across different languages and cultures.

What is the International Space Station (ISS)?

572. The ISS is a global project where scientists from 15 countries live and work together in space. It's a symbol of international cooperation in science.

573. The ISS makes 16 orbits around Earth each day, traveling at a speed of 17,500 miles per hour!

574. Ibn al-Haytham (Iraq) invented the camera obscura, a step toward modern cameras. Can you remember his work with optics from the physics chapter?

575. Chien-Shiung Wu (China/USA) proved some big physics ideas with tiny atoms.

Interactive Activity: Who Did What?

Match these scientists to their feats.

(1) Ibn al-Haytham	(a) Radioactivity
(2) Marie Curie	(b) Camera obscura
(3) Wu	(c) Atom experiments

The right answers: 1-b, 2-a, 3-c)

How many did you get correctly? Kudos!

Sub-section 2.2: Bilingual STEM Learning

How can learning science in two languages help you?

576. Learning science in two languages helps you understand concepts better and lets you communicate with people from different cultures. It also makes your brain stronger.

577. Bilingual students frequently excel in math and science since they are accustomed to approaching problems from various angles.

578. 'Water' can be 'agua' (Spanish), 'eau' (French), or '水' (Mandarin) depending on where you are at the moment.

579. The word 'chemistry' comes from the Arabic word 'al-kīmiyā.'

580. 'Gravity' in Spanish is 'gravedad.'

581. 'Electricity' in French is 'électricité.'

582. 'Photosynthesis' in Mandarin is '光合作用 (guāng hé zuò yòng).'

583. The term 'science' originates from the Latin 'scientia,' translating to 'knowledge.'

584. 'Energy' in Mandarin is Néngyuán.

585. 'Robot' in Japanese is 'robotto'—sounds familiar, huh?

586. Many science museums around the world offer exhibits and programs in multiple languages to make science accessible to everyone.

How do scientists communicate across languages?

587. Scientists use universal symbols, equations, and diagrams to share ideas. They also translate their work into multiple languages so people everywhere can learn from it.

588. The periodic table is the same in every language because it uses symbols, like 'H' for hydrogen and 'O' for oxygen.

Interactive Activity: Bilingual Flashcards

Create flashcards with English scientific words on one side and the same words in other global languages on the other side. Here are some word pairs to consider *'evaporation'* and *'evaporación.' 'gravity'* and *'gravedad.'*

Sub-section 2.3: Building a Global STEM Community

589. The Internet allows scientists to share ideas and work together no matter where they are.

590. Scientists share their plans, findings and reports through entries in scientific journals where other scientists can read them.

591. Many families now start their own science clubs at home, where each member picks a topic to explore and share with the family to improve their scientific knowledge.

592. Families can join online platforms like SciStarter or Zooniverse to share experiments, participate in citizen science projects, and connect with others around the world.

593. There are over 2 million volunteers on Zooniverse helping scientists to analyze data, such as classifying galaxies or tracking wildlife.

594. International science competitions can also bring students from different countries together to compete and learn from each other.

595. Doing science experiments together, like making slime or building a volcano, can be a fun way for families to bond.

What are citizen science projects?

596. Citizen science projects are opportunities for people of all ages to help with real scientific research. For example, you can count birds in your backyard for the Great Backyard Bird Count.

597. Every February, the Great Backyard Bird Count engages participants from more than 100 countries.

598. Kids can share their experiments and discoveries on social media, blogs, or science fair websites. They can also join global challenges like the Google Science Fair.

599. The Google Science Fair has had winners from countries like India, the USA, and Kenya. This shows that great ideas can come from anywhere.

What is the ISEF?

600. The International Science and Engineering Fair (ISEF) is the largest global science competition for high school students. Some past winners of the ISEF have also gone on to win Nobel Prizes.

601. ISEF brings together over 1,800 students from 80+ countries every year to showcase their projects.

Interactive Activity: Join a Global Stem Challenge

Join an online global STEM challenge, like the NASA Space Apps Challenge, and work with a team to solve a real-world problem.

Section 3: Global Scientist Spotlight – Everyday Innovators

Sub-section 3.1: Modern Role Models in STEM

602. Dr. Mae Jemison was the first African American woman to travel to space. She's also a doctor, engineer, and advocate for science education.

603. After retiring from NASA, Dr. Jemison started the Dorothy Jemison Foundation to inspire kids to pursue STEM careers.

Who is Dr. Hadiyah-Nicole Green?

604. Dr. Hadiyah-Nicole Green is a physicist who developed a laser treatment for cancer. She's one of the first African-American women to earn a Ph.D. in physics.

605. Dr. Green's treatment uses lasers to target cancer cells without harming healthy tissue, making it less painful than traditional treatments.

Who is Dr. Jane Goodall?

606. Dr. Jane Goodall is a primatologist who studied chimpanzees in Tanzania. Her work changed how we understand animals and conservation.

607. Dr. Goodall started the Roots & Shoots program to empower young people to protect the environment.

Who is Dr. Temple Grandin?

608. Dr. Temple Grandin is an animal scientist and autism advocate. She designed humane systems for handling livestock and has written books about autism and animal behavior.

609. Dr. Grandin's designs are used in over half of the cattle facilities in the United States.

610. Dr. Youyou Tu of China discovered a treatment for malaria, saving millions of lives.

611. Dr. Kizzmekia Corbett of the USA helped to make a COVID-19 vaccine fast.

612. Dr. Fei-Fei Li works on teaching AI to see and process images better and faster.

613. Elon Musk's SpaceX rockets go to space and come back to Earth. He's making space travel awesome. He is also a leading manufacturer of electric vehicles.

614. Dr. Akira Yoshino worked heavily to help us develop the lithium-ion battery in our smart-phones.

615. Greta Thunberg is a young climate advocate who has motivated many to take action for the environment.

Interactive Activity: Choose a Hero!

Choose a modern scientist from above and create a poster about their life and work. Find out new details that have not been discussed above and include them in the poster.

Sub-section 3.2: Stories from Your Community

Who are the innovators in your neighborhood?

616. Look around! Your community might have engineers, teachers, or even kids who are solving problems and inventing new things.

617. Many famous inventors, like Thomas Edison and Steve Jobs, started tinkering in their garages as kids.

How can you learn from local scientists?

618. Visit science museums, attend local science fairs, or join a STEM club at school. You can also interview a scientist or engineer in your community.

619. Science fairs often have judges who are local scientists and engineers. They love to share their knowledge with young innovators.

What are some community STEM projects?

620. Examples of some community STEM projects include building gardens, creating recycling programs, or even designing apps to solve local problems.

621. In Kenya, students built a solar-powered water purification system to provide clean water for their village.

How can you inspire others with your STEM ideas?

622. You can inspire others by sharing your experiments and inventions with friends, family, and your school. You can also post videos or write articles to inspire others.

623. Many young inventors have started YouTube channels to share their projects, such as building robots or creating eco-friendly gadgets.

624. Your phone has science (camera), tech (apps), engineering (design), and math (coding). It's STEM in your pocket!

Interactive Activity: STEM Day!

Organize a STEM day at your school or community center. Invite local scientists to share their work and host hands-on activities.

Sub-section 3.3: Lighting the Spark for Future Innovators

How can you become a young innovator?

625. Start by asking questions, experimenting, and solving problems. Join STEM clubs, enter competitions, and never stop being curious!

626. Many famous scientists, like Albert Einstein and Marie Curie, started as curious kids who loved to explore the world.

What are some global STEM challenges for kids like you?

627. There are many challenges, like the Google Science Fair, FIRST Robotics, and the NASA Space Apps Challenge. These competitions let kids solve real-world problems and share their ideas with the world.

628. The FIRST Robotics competition has over 600,000 participants from more than one hundred countries every year.

How can you document your STEM adventures?

629. Keep a science journal, take photos, or make videos of your experiments. Consider starting a blog to showcase your findings.

630. Many young scientists have turned their journals into books or YouTube channels, inspiring others to explore STEM.

Interactive Activity : Join a Challenge!

Either join a global science challenge or start your own STEM project. Share your journey with the world and inspire others to explore the wonders of science.

Chapter Takeaways

- Science turns everyday stuff—like baking soda or paper—into awesome experiments!

- Everyday moments are full of STEM adventures, from kitchen experiments to backyard physics.
- Learning science in multiple languages and celebrating global diversity makes STEM more fun and inclusive.
- Modern scientists and local innovators inspire us to dream big and solve real-world problems.
- You can become a young innovator by asking questions, experimenting, and sharing your ideas with the world.

Chapter 7: Digital Intelligence – AI, ChatGPT, and the Future of Learning

Imagine conversing with a digital mind that not only answers your questions but sparks new ideas in every language.

What if machines could think, learn, and create alongside humans? How would that change the way we explore the world?

Did you know that AI can now recognize faces with 99% accuracy—better than most humans? And tools like ChatGPT can write essays, code, and jokes in over 50 languages!

Section 1: The Rise of Artificial Intelligence

Sub-section 1.1: Early Dreams and Foundational Theories

From Turing's groundbreaking ideas to early computer pioneers, AI's roots run deep.

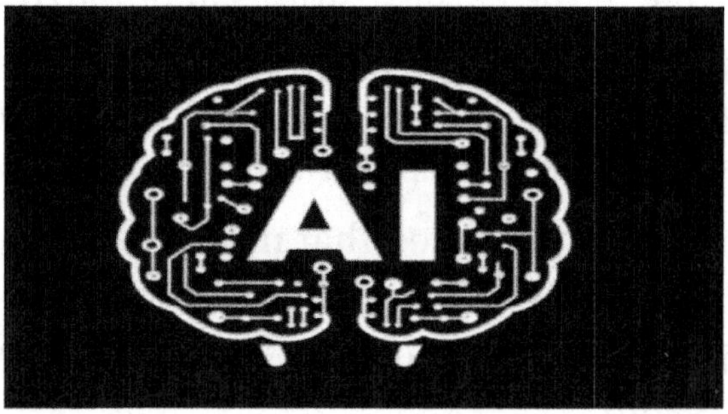

What is artificial intelligence (AI)?

631. Artificial intelligence allows machines to undertake tasks typically associated with human intelligence, like learning, solving problems, and comprehending language.

632. 'Artificial intelligence' was first mentioned in 1956 at a conference at Dartmouth College in the USA.

633. Alan Turing, a brilliant British mathematician, imagined machines that could solve problems and even hold conversations like humans.

634. In 1950, Turing proposed the famous Turing Test, which basically asks “can a machine answer questions so naturally that you can’t tell it’s not human?”

635. Turing’s ideas were so influential that many computer programs today still follow principles he described over 70 years ago.

636. Alan Turing also helped the Allies to win World War II by cracking secret codes with machines. This helped the Allies to intercept and understand the enemy’s plan.

637. No AI has completely passed the Turing Test yet but recent developments like ChatGPT have come close.

Did ancient people dream of AI or something similar?

638. "Yes! Ancient myths and stories often featured mechanical beings. For example, the ancient Greeks built automatons (self-moving machines), and 9th-century inventors in Baghdad designed programmable musical robots.

639. The Greek myth of Talos, a giant bronze robot that guarded the island of Crete, is one of the earliest stories about artificial beings.

640. Ada Lovelace was a 19th-century scientist who wrote the first computer algorithm for a machine that didn’t even exist yet! She is often called the world’s first computer programmer.

641. Ada Lovelace also predicted that machines would one day create music and art. That is something AI tools can do today.

642. In Spanish, ‘inteligencia’ means intelligence. Practice saying it *‘in-tell-ee-HEN-see-ah!’*

Interactive Activity: AI Milestones

Arrange these important AI milestones in order of when they occurred, starting from the earliest.

A. Lady Ada Lovelace writes the first algorithm

B. Alan Turing introduces the Turing Test

C. ChatGPT is launched

D. Ancient Greeks build automatons

What do you have?

The right order is DABC. Did you get it right?

Sub-section 1.2: Breakthroughs in Machine Learning

What is machine learning?

643. Machine learning, ML, is the way computers learn from data rather than being programmed step-by-step. It is a way of teaching computers to learn from examples, like how you learn by practicing.

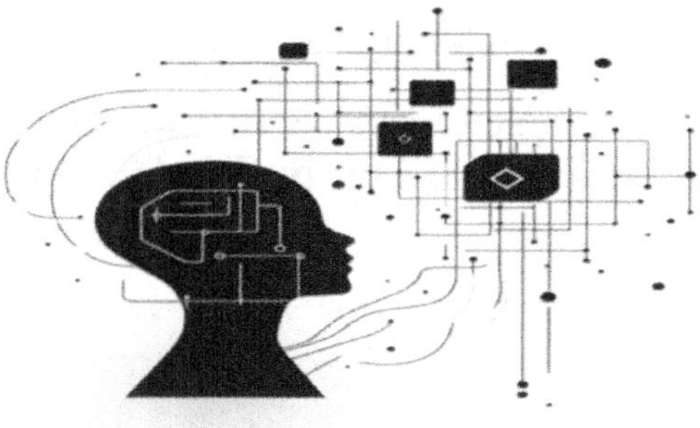

644. Machine learning algorithms have improved over time. For instance, Netflix employs machine learning to suggest shows that align with your preferences. The same applies to platforms like X (formerly Twitter), Instagram and Facebook.

645. Online marketplaces also use ML algorithms to recommend the right product based on previous orders, location, and search history of the user

What are neural networks?

646. Neural networks are computer systems inspired by the biological structure of the human brain. They consist of layers of neurons that process information and learn patterns, like recognizing faces or translating languages.

647. The first neural networks were built in the 1980s.

648. The human brain contains roughly 86 billion neurons, while a neural network might have millions or even billions of artificial neurons.

649. Early computer programs could only follow simple instructions, but neural networks enabled computers to 'learn' and adapt on their own.

650. Early chatbots like ELIZA (1966) could only mimic therapists by repeating questions. ChatGPT is 10,000x smarter!

651. In 2016, Google's AlphaGo AI beat the world champion at Go, a game with more possible moves than atoms in the universe! This was a huge milestone in AI history.

652. Go is so complex that even the best human players can't predict every move. The game is much more complex than chess.

653. AlphaGo used machine learning to master the game in just a few years and defeated the human champion. Impressive!

654. Yoshua Bengio (Canada), Yann LeCun (France), and Geoffrey Hinton (UK) are known as the 'Godfathers of AI' for their groundbreaking work on deep learning, a type of machine learning.

655. In 2019, these three scientists won the Turing Award, which is also known as the 'Nobel Prize of Computing,' for their contributions to AI.

656. Deep learning is like giving AI x-ray vision to spot patterns in pictures or words.

657. Deep learning, a modern type of neural network, uses many layers (sometimes called 'deep' layers) to process data and make decisions.

658. It takes tons of examples—for example, showing AI 10,000 dog pics to learn what a dog looks like.

659. Fei-Fei Li from China launched the ImageNet dataset in 2009. This revolutionized computer vision by providing millions of labeled images for training AI.

660. In Brazil, AI helps translate old Portuguese stories. Machine learning loves languages.

661. Training ChatGPT took enough energy to power 1,000 homes for a year.

Interactive Insight: AI Matching Game

I want you to match the following three AI inventions (in the left column) to their correct country of origin (in the right column).

Self-driving cars	Japan
Robot Chefs	China
Facial recognition	USA/Germany

Now, go online and try to find out if you got the correct pairs.

Sub-section 1.3: The Global Impact of AI

Today, AI touches every aspect of life—from healthcare to transportation.

What role is AI playing in agriculture?

662. In India, AI-powered apps help farmers predict monsoons, choose the best crops, and avoid pests. This helps them grow more food and earn more money.

663. Plantix, an AI app, can diagnose plant diseases just by looking at a photo of a leaf. Incredible!

664. In Kenya, AI drones fly over farms to check if plants need water.

Can AI help with mental health?

665. Yes! AI chatbots like Woebot (USA) provide mental health support to teens in 10+ languages. They offer advice, track moods, and even teach coping skills.

666. Woebot uses natural language processing (NLP) to understand and respond to users' feelings. That's just like a regular human therapist!

How is AI used in schools?"

667. In South Korea, AI robots teach English in schools. They can correct pronunciation, answer questions, and even play games with students.

668. Some AI tutoring apps adapt lessons to each student's learning style, making education more personalized and effective.

669. In Germany, AI helps us to improve self-driving cars. AI can watch the road and make safety-based decisions for you.

670. In healthcare, AI can help us to analyze medical images, draw conclusions and improve the prediction of the course of a disease.

671. In Japan, AI robots are used in elderly care, addressing aging population challenges.

672. AI is also in use in the entertainment world as algorithms that recommend the right movie or music to users. Spotify and Youtube are great examples of this.

673. AI-powered translation applications like Duolingo can help you understand other languages better from the comfort of your house.

Are there any challenges in the use of AI?

674. AI can sometimes make mistakes or be biased. For example, early facial recognition systems struggled to recognize darker skin tones. Scientists are working to make AI better and more accurate.

675. The European Union created the first AI law to ban harmful uses, like social profiling and discrimination, and to ensure AI is used responsibly.

Interactive Activity: Pick the Right Tool

a) IBM Watson

b) Google Translate

c) The Ocean Cleanup's AI drones

There are three AI tools above. Which one of them would you choose to,

1. Detect a rare disease

2. Translate a Japanese comic

3. Get rid of plastic in the ocean

What are your answers? The correct answer is 1. (A), 2. (B) and 3. (C). They were already in the right order.

Section 2: ChatGPT and the Evolution of Language Models

Sub-section 2.1: The Birth of ChatGPT

ChatGPT emerged as a breakthrough in conversational AI, transforming how we interact with machines.

What is ChatGPT?

676. ChatGPT is an AI language model created by OpenAI. It can write stories, solve riddles, and even write an essay all by predicting the next word in a sentence.

677. ChatGPT was trained on billions of books, websites, and conversations. It's like a super-smart parrot that learns from everything it reads.

678. ChatGPT is based on a transformer model, a type of neural network that revolutionized AI in 2017.

679. ChatGPT was created by OpenAI, a company with teams from 30+ countries. Their goal is to make AI safe and helpful for everyone.

680. OpenAI's co-founders include Elon Musk and Sam Altman. They believe AI should benefit humanity and not harm it.

681. OpenAI started and operated as a not-for-profit organization but there have been recent controversial moves to change that status.

What can ChatGPT do?

682. ChatGPT can write essays, code, jokes, and even poems. It is also good at translating languages and can help with homework.

683. ChatGPT is part of a large family called GPT, Generative Pretrained Transformers.

684. The first GPT, GPT-1, was launched in 2018 and could only write simple sentences like "The cat is cute."

685. GPT-2 in 2019 showed advanced text generation with close to 1.5 billion parameters.

686. By 2020, GPT-3 with 175 billion parameters could write essays and even make up jokes but it did not generate much attention from the mainstream public.

687. ChatGPT finally arrived in 2022, ready to chat and help with work, and dominated the headlines for months thereafter.

688. ChatGPT speaks many languages! It can say 'hello"' in French (bonjour), Hindi (namaste), and at least 93 more languages.

689. ChatGPT is very fast and typically answers queries in a few seconds.

690. ChatGPT can even perform complex programming tasks such as debugging and writing code.

691. Recently, there has been development of tools similar to ChatGPT. A team from China unleashed DeepSeek AI. Grok AI is another alternative.

692. The Transformer Model used in ChatGPT was first used in Google Translate.

Interactive Activity: Find a Task for ChatGPT

Get a sheet of paper. Now, start to make a list of the things you can use ChatGPT for. Write down at least ten!

Sub-section 2.2: How ChatGPT Works

Behind the friendly AI conversation lies a complex network of neural computations.

693. ChatGPT splits your words into tokens—tiny pieces like "I" "like" "to" "run." Tokens are numbered for the AI to process, like a secret code.

694. Then, ChatGPT uses attention mechanisms to focus on what matters most in your question.

695. Based on mathematical prediction, it guesses the next word, building answers one step at a time.

What are tokens?

696. Little word bits that ChatGPT uses to understand you. They are like Lego bricks for sentences.

697. A token can be as short as one letter or as long as a word. For example, 'ChatGPT' is one token, but 'artificial intelligence' is two.

What are attention mechanisms?"

698. Attention mechanisms help ChatGPT focus on the most important words in a sentence. It's like how you pay attention to your teacher's voice in a noisy classroom.

699. Attention mechanisms were introduced in 2017 and revolutionized AI. They are the secret of why ChatGPT can understand long, complicated sentences.

How does ChatGPT learn?

700. ChatGPT learns by reading billions of books, websites, and conversations. It uses this data to predict what words come next in a sentence.

701. Training ChatGPT was energy-intensive. Scientists from across the globe are trying hard to make AI more energy-efficient.

Can ChatGPT make mistakes?

702. Yes! ChatGPT can make mistakes because it doesn't truly understand language. Instead, it just predicts words based on patterns. Therefore, sometimes it gives silly or wrong answers!

Interactive Activity: ChatGPT Inner Workings Quiz

Put these steps of how ChatGPT works in the right order

A. Tokenize the question.

B. Pick the best one.

C. Rank answers by likelihood.

D. Generate possible answers.

What have you got?

The right order is ADCB!

Sub-section 2.3: Ethical Considerations and Future Prospects

As AI grows smarter, ethical challenges and transformative possibilities emerge. AI is good but we have to use it right

703. Privacy is a concern with AI tools. Users are being encouraged not to share very deep secrets with AI tools

Can AI be biased?

704. Yes, this can happen. AI can exhibit bias when trained on flawed data. AI relies a lot on the initial data that is fed in.

705. This potential bias can be reduced by diverse training data, which is a global effort.

706. Companies like IBM are now training AI on diverse datasets to make it fairer and more accurate.

707. Quantum computing could make AI solve problems in minutes, not years.

What are the risks involved in the use of AI?"

708. AI can be used in harmful ways, like spreading fake news or invading privacy. Therefore, it is very important to create laws and guidelines to ensure AI is used responsibly.

How can AI help preserve cultures?

709. AI helps in safeguarding endangered languages and cultural practices. For example, Indigenous communities in Australia are using AI to record and translate their languages.

710. There are over 7,000 languages in the world, and nearly half are at risk of disappearing. AI could help save most of them!

What is the future of AI ethics?

711. The future of AI ethics involves creating fair, transparent, and accountable systems. Scientists, governments, and communities must work together to ensure AI benefits everyone.

712. Some countries, like Canada and Finland, are teaching AI ethics in schools to prepare the next generation for the challenges of AI.

713. In the future, AI might also help us to reduce pollution and reverse climate change

714. International frameworks like UNESCO's AI ethics guidelines are still being developed.

715. The first AI ethics conference occurred in 2017.

716. Some countries, such as Canada, have AI ethics boards to oversee the development of AI in a way that will be safe for everyone.

Interactive Activity: Pros vs. Cons Debate

Draw two columns on a sheet of paper and label them as 'pros' and 'cons.' Try to list some of the benefits and advantages of AI under the 'pros' column and list some of its possible dangers in the 'cons' column. Which column has more items?

Section 3: AI in Everyday Life and Beyond

Sub-section 3.1: AI as a Personal and Educational Assistant

Smart devices and virtual assistants are making everyday life and learning more efficient.

Can AI help you with your homework and research projects?

717. AI tools like ChatGPT can explain math problems, write essays, and even quiz you on history. It'slike having a tutor available for your needs 24/7.

718. Duolingo's AI tutors adapt lessons to your mistakes and are always available—like a teacher who never sleeps or goes home.

719. AI tools can set mock examinations, complete summaries of books, and write short prose for you.

720. AI can also help teachers and tutors to grade assignments and examinations faster and more fairly.

721. For an AI tool to work properly, you must prompt it the right way.

722. A prompt is a set of unique and detailed instructions given to an AI tool to guide its work. The output you'll get depends on the prompt you give the tool.

723. Some people work as prompt engineers. They design instructions for very complex tasks.

Can AI help people with disabilities to learn better?

724. Yes! For instance, in Brazil, AI apps help blind students 'see' diagrams through sound. The app describes the image, allowing students to learn just like their friends.

725. AI-powered prosthetics can now be controlled by thought, allowing people with disabilities to move robotic limbs with their minds.

How is AI used in smart homes?

726. AI tools can recognize your voice and follow your commands. That makes them important as virtual, home, and personal assistants.

727. AI powers smart home devices like Alexa and Google Home. They can play the music you want, control all your lights, and even order groceries with voice commands.

728. Some smart fridges use AI to track expiration dates and suggest recipes based on what's inside the fridges.

729. Virtual reality (VR) powered by AI can take you on interactive field trips. With VR powered by AI you can visit a museum or the Taj Mahal right from your classroom.

What are the challenges of AI in education?

730. AI can sometimes give wrong answers or make students rely too much on technology. So, it's important to use AI as a tool, not a replacement for learning. Do not cheat by using AI when it is prohibited.

731. In South Africa, AI is being used to turn textbooks into audiobooks for kids.

732. In Mexico, AI translates school lessons into languages like Nahuatl.

733. AI is often used in map applications like Google and Apple Maps. So, it is correct to say AI can tell your parents the fastest way to soccer practice.

734. Some toys and online chatbots use AI to talk back to you—like a chatty teddy bear!

Interactive Activity: Spot the AI!

Now that you know a lot about AI and its uses, I want you to look around you and give examples of AI at work.

Alexa setting a timer, Netflix recommending a show, and your mom's weather app are all AI; how many more examples were you able to spot?

Sub-section 3.2: Digital Creativity and Art

AI is not just analytical—it's also a powerful creative partner.

735. AI can analyze thousands of pieces of art, songs, and poems to learn different styles. AI can then mix these ideas to create original art, compose new music, or even write new stories and poems.

736. An AI-generated portrait sold for $432,500 at Christie's auction house in 2018. Critics called it the 'Robot Renaissance.'

737. *Midjourney* and several other AI tools have the ability to create pictures based on a prompt.

How can AI help with creative writing?

738. A creative writer's best friends are new ideas. In this regard, AI can help. AI can suggest story ideas, help structure narratives, check for plot holes, and offer dialogue suggestions.

739. Musicians are now using AI to experiment with new sounds, creating unique compositions that blend different musical traditions.

740. AIVA was the first virtual composer recognized by a music society. It has composed over 1,000 pieces of classical music.

741. There are online platforms where you can collaborate with AI to create a story or a piece of music in real time.

742. ChatGPT can write poems in Arabic or songs in Spanish—pretty cool.

743. Kids like you can team up with AI to draw wild creatures or any other thing that catches your fancy.

Can AI write books?

744. Yes! ChatGPT can write a book that is several hundred pages long—but it will still need human editors to make it perfect.

Will AI eventually replace human artists and musicians?

745. Nobody is sure! However, humans will always be needed to prompt AI tools and review the output from these tools.

746. Some authors use AI to brainstorm ideas or edit their work, but most agree that AI can't replace human creativity. For now!

What are the limits of AI creativity?

747. AI can mimic creativity but doesn't truly 'feel' emotions or understand art. It relies on patterns in data, not personal experiences. So, its output can feel a bit cold sometimes or lack the human touch.

748. Smart artists see AI as a tool and not a rival. They may just be right!

Interactive Activity: Real or AI-Made?

Search "AI art" online. Pick a picture that is made by AI.

Are there any notable differences between it and human-made art?

In what way does it look different from human-made art?

Can you tell AI and human-made art apart easily?

Sub-section 3.3: The Future Frontier: Beyond ChatGPT

The journey of digital intelligence is only beginning, with endless possibilities on the horizon. We have not even scratched the surface of what it can do yet.

What is general AI?

749. General AI is a type of AI that can think and learn like a human. Unlike ChatGPT, which is specialized, general AI could perform any intellectual task.

750. General AI doesn't exist yet, but scientists are working on it. Some predict it could be achieved by 2050.

751. Quantum computers could make AI a million times faster and better. Amazing!

752. Many experts believe that future AI will not only help us learn and work but also address worldwide issues like climate change, health crises, and resource management.

How could AI help in space exploration?

753. NASA's AI pilots could someday steer spaceships to distant planets. AI could also analyze data from telescopes to find signs of alien life.

754. AI is already helping NASA map the surfaces of Mars and the Moon. That will make it easier for future astronauts to explore.

755. Scientists are training AI to design new medicines in weeks instead of years.

Could AI help us talk to animals?

756. Yes! Scientists are using AI to decode animal communication, like whale songs and dolphin clicks.

757. AI has already helped to decode prairie dog calls, which vary depending on the type of predator near them.

758. AI might also play a role in helping to clear the oceans of plastic waste.

What are the risks of advanced AI?

759. Advanced AI could be used in harmful ways, like creating fake videos or controlling weapons.

760. Some scientists, including Stephen Hawking, warn that advanced AI could pose risks to humanity if not controlled carefully.

Interactive Activity: Make Your AI Pick!

Which AI advancement and potential AI future excites you most?

1. Robot friends and assistants
2. Homework-solving AI
3. AI that can talk to animals
4. AI helping us to discover alien life in space

Chapter Takeaways

- AI began with ancient myths and evolved into tools like ChatGPT that can write, learn, and create.
- Machine learning lets AI improve by practicing—just like you do with math problems.
- ChatGPT chats and learns from a huge pile of words!
- The future of AI could include robot doctors, intergalactic explorers, and even whale translators!
- AI is already in your life, making school, art, and fun even better.
- The future's bright, but we've got to keep AI fair and friendly for all.

Chapter 8: Global Innovators – Scientists and Inventors Who Changed the World

Have you ever wondered who invented the technology that lets you talk to people across the world? Or who first discovered life-saving medicines?

Behind every great invention is a curious mind that dared to explore the unknown. Science and innovation are not limited to one place or time—they come from every culture and era.

Section 1: Historical Pioneers

Sub-section 1.1: Trailblazers of Antiquity

761. Ancient innovators laid the groundwork for modern science. You have already met some of them and their work in earlier chapters.

762. The Incas built suspension bridges from grass ropes that could hold hundreds of people.

763. The Babylonians created the first written laws (Hammurabi's Code) and studied the stars to predict seasons.

764. The Chinese invented paper, gunpowder, and the compass. These inventions all changed the world forever!

765. The Romans were smart builders. They built aqueducts to carry water across cities, using gravity, and developed precise engineering.

766. The Incas built Machu Picchu with perfectly-cut stones.

767. The Polynesians used stars and ocean currents to navigate thousands of miles across the Pacific.

768. The Aztecs built floating gardens (chinampas) to grow food on lakes.

769. The Persians learned to build windmills to grind grain and pump water.

770. The Arabs invented distillation to make perfumes and medicines, and improve navigation tools like the astrolabe.

771. The Mayan Long Count calendar, developed in the third century BCE, was so accurate that it could predict astronomical events thousands of years in the future.

772. In Africa, the Kingdom of Kush (Sudan) built advanced iron tools and weapons.

773. Ancient African metallurgists also developed advanced iron smelting techniques.

Who was Imhotep, and why is he important?

774. Imhotep was an ancient Egyptian polymath who lived around 2600 BCE. He was an architect, physician, and engineer, and he designed the Step Pyramid of Djoser, the world's first large stone building.

775. Imhotep is often called the 'Father of Medicine' because he wrote some of the earliest medical texts that described treatments for over 200 diseases

776. Mansa Musa, often regarded as the richest-ever man, was a patron of learning and science in Mali.

777. Ibn Ridwan (988-1061CE) was an Egyptian physician and astrologer, who wrote on medical astrology.

778. Abd al-Rahman al-Sufi (903-986CE) was an influential astronomer in Africa who cataloged stars.

779. Al-Biruni (973-1048CE) was an early authority on astronomy and geography in Africa.

Remember Zheng Heng? He wasn't the only amazing Chinese scientist.

780. He was the Chinese scientist who invented the first seismoscope to detect earthquakes hundreds of miles away.

781. Zhang Heng's seismoscope, invented in the second century CE, used a pendulum and bronze balls to indicate the direction of an earthquake.

782. Zhang Heng's seismoscope was so advanced that similar devices weren't developed in Europe until the 19th century, almost 17 centuries later!

783. Sun Zi was a Chinese mathematician who wrote *The Mathematical Manual of the Five Administrations,* including the "Chinese Remainder Theorem."

784. Su Song (1020-1101 CE) built a water-powered astronomical clock, a marvel of engineering.

785. Yang Shen (1488-1559CE) was a scholar of astronomy and mathematics and he contributed to celestial observations.

786. Li Shizhen (1518-1593CE) was a pharmacist who wrote the *Compendium of Materia Medica,* a guide on herbs and medicines.

787. Song Yingxing (1587-1666CE) wrote the*Exploitation of the Works of Nature*, a book that covered various technologies.

788. Xuanzang (602-664CE) was a Chinese monk who brought Buddhist texts and knowledge from India to China, influencing science.

789. In India, Aryabhata (476 CE) calculated pi, mathematical constants and explained eclipses.

790. Sshruta, the Father of Surgeries, was performing surgeries, including plastic surgeries, in India 2,600 years ago.

791. In the second century, Charaka, a physician, wrote *Charaka Samhita*, a foundational text of Ayurvedic medicine.

792. In that same century, Nagarjuna, a chemist and alchemist, wrote *Rasaratnakara*, discussing mercury and its compounds.

793. Brahmagupta (598-668 CE) wrote *Brahmasphuta Siddhanta* on arithmetic and algebra.

What role did Middle Eastern scientists play?

794. Ibn al-Haytham (Iraq, 965 - 1040 CE) laid the groundwork that helped us build the first camera.

795. Al-Jazari lived between 1136 and 1206. He is credited with inventing automated machines, including water pumps and mechanical clocks.

796. The Persian, Al-Khwarizmi (780–850 CE) invented algebra and wrote *The Compendious Book on Calculation.*

797. Al-Razi (865-925 CE) was a chemist and physician who wrote *The Virtuous Life*, which included observations on smallpox and measles.

798. Omar Khayyam (1048-1131 CE) A mathematician and poet, worked on algebra and calendar reform.

799. Al-Biruni (973-1048 CE) wrote about astronomy, mathematics, and geography, and he also tried to measure the Earth's circumference.

800. Jabir ibn Hayyan (721-815 CE) was known as the 'Father of Chemistry' in Islam, and discovered many chemical processes like distillation.

801. Al-Farabi (872-950 CE) was a philosopher and scientist who was known as the "Second Teacher" after Aristotle.

802. Ibn Yunus (950-1009 CE) compiled astronomical tables used for centuries in navigation.

803. Al-Masudi (896-956 CE) was a geographer and historian who wrote about the world's cultures and sciences, influencing geography.

804. Ibn Sinna (980-1037 CE) more commonly known as Avicenna in the West wrote *The Book of The Cure*, a medical encyclopedia used for centuries in Europe.

The Greeks were not to be left behind!

805. Eratosthenes calculated Earth's circumference.

806. Archimedes of Syracuse was the first recorded person to attempt to calculate the mathematical value of pi. He used a method that involved polygons.

807. Hypatia was a Greek mathematician, astronomer, and philosopher who lived in the 4th century CE. She was one of the first women to make significant contributions to science and mathematics and she invented the astrolabe.

808. For 1000 years, the astrolabe was essential for navigation and astronomy.

809. The pythagorean theorem was the result of hard work from the Greek Pythagoras. The theorem is still in use today.

810. Ptolemy (90-168 AD) created the geocentric model and the first world map.

811. Galen (129-216 AD) wrote extensively on anatomy and physiology and he influenced medical thought for many centuries.

812. Euclid (325-265 BC), a famous mathematician, wrote the *Elements of Geometry* that contains valuable information still taught today.

813. Thales of Miletus (624-546 BC) certainly caught many people by surprise when he correctly predicted a solar eclipse.

814. Pliny the Elder (23-79 AD), a naturalist, wrote *Natural History*, documenting natural phenomena.

Interactive Activity: Who Came First?

Arrange these ancient innovators in order.

A. Imhotep (2600 BCE)

B. Zhang Heng (2nd century CE)

C. Al Razi (865-925 CE)

D. Hypatia (4th century CE)

The right order is ABDC.

Sub-section 1.2: The Renaissance and Enlightenment

During the Renaissance, cultural rebirth sparked scientific innovations that changed the world.

815. ‘Renaissance’ means ‘rebirth’ in French.

816. The Renaissance was a period between the 14th and 17th centuries marked by European cultural, artistic, political, and economic resurgence.

817. During the Renaissance, there was a re-awakening of interest in the arts, literature, and philosophy of ancient Greece and Rome.

818. During the Renaissance, wealthy and influential families like the Medicis of Florence became patrons of artists and scientists.

819. The Renaissance inspired trade, exploration and voyages. This resulted in the identification of new trade routes and innovations.

820. Before the Renaissance, the church was in charge of the political and religious landscapes of Europe.

821. The Renaissance encouraged a shift in power from the church and traditional systems to science. More nation states also developed.

822. Florence, Italy was at the center of the Renaissance before it spread to other notable European cities.

Who was Leonardo da Vinci? And what about other famous European Renaissance innovators?

823. Leonardo da Vinci was an Italian polymath who lived during the Renaissance. He was an artist, scientist, and inventor, known for his sketches of flying machines, submarines, and human anatomy.

824. Leonardo's designs for a flying machine were inspired by the wings of birds. While he never built it, his ideas laid the groundwork for modern aviation.

825. Sir Isaac Newton is probably the most famous scientist of the Renaissance. His work was spread across the fields of motion, optics, and gravity.

826. Galileo Galilei, an Italian astronomer, identified the moons of Jupiter, the phases of Venus, and the Moon's craters.

827. Today, Galileo is celebrated as one of the fathers of modern science but back then he was persecuted for daring to propose such *radical* beliefs.

828. Nicholas Copernicus was a Polish astronomer who also suggested that the sun was at the center of our solar system.

829. Antoine Lavoisier of France named several elements, including oxygen.

830. Rene Descartes, a French philosopher and mathematician, created analytical geometry. That allowed Sir Newton to discover calculus.

831. Johannes Kepler, a German astronomer, suggested some laws of planetary motion.

832. Robert Boyle was an Irish scientist that gave us Boyle's Law. This law outlines how pressure relates to the volume of a gas.

833. Robert Hooke, an English scientist, made huge strides in the fields of physics and biology. He was the first to confirm the existence of cells. He also worked in the field of elasticity and gave the world Hooke's law.

834. Antoine Leeuwenhoeke worked on the identification of microorganisms and was the first to see bacteria under the microscope

835. Johannes Gutenberg invented the printing press in 1400. That made it practical to print books and disseminate information on a large scale.

836. Paracelsus was a chemist and physician who worked extensively in the field of toxicology to explain the dose-effect relationship.

837. Christopher Columbus discovered the New World in the 15th century while he was trying to find a direct water route to Asia.

838. Blaise Pascal developed the first mechanical calculator.

839. Christiaan Huygens was a Dutch astronomer who discovered Saturn's rings and invented the pendulum clock.

840. William Harvey, an Englishman, was the first to accurately describe our cardiovascular system.

841. Evangelista Torricelli invented the barometer to measure air pressure.

842. Benjamin Franklin also gave the world the gift of electricity.

843. In England, Edmond Halley predicted the return of the comet named after him, Halley's comet

844. Alessandro Volta created the first practical batteries.

845. Joseph Black discovered carbon dioxide and called it fixed air.

846. In 1774, Joseph Priestley (1733–1804) discovered oxygen from the decomposition of mercuric oxide.

847. James Cook was an explorer who discovered a lot about the Pacific Ocean and mapped new lands.

848. James Watt from Scotland made improvements to the steam engine.

849. Carolus Linnaeus was a Swede who introduced the Binomial nomenclature for naming species on land and in water.

850. Maria Sibylla Merian, (1647–1717), a German, pioneered the study of insects and their life cycles.

851. Andreas Vesalius (1514-1564) published *De Humani Corporis Fabrica,* and is often regarded as the 'Father of Modern Anatomy.'

852. Tycho Brahe (1546-1601) made accurate planetary observations without using a telescope.

853. Edward Jenner was one of the pioneers of vaccination after developing the vaccine for smallpox.

854. Mary Anning, a paleontologist, found important fossils that contributed to geology.

855. Caroline Herschel (1750-1848) was a brilliant astronomer who discovered comets.

856. Adam Smith (1723-1790) is one of the most famous names in economic science. He wrote *The Wealth of Nations,* a text that is still valuable today!

857. Humphry Davy discovered potassium and sodium, important elements, and body electrolytes, in the 19th century.

858. Denis Diderot (1713-1784) was responsible for the editing of the *Encyclopédie.*

859. Nicolaus Otto, a German, was responsible for the first modern internal combustion engine built in 1876.

Interactive Activity: Linking Inventions to Their Inventors

Link the inventions in the left column to the correct inventors in the right column.

1. Smallpox vaccine	A. Johannes Gutenberg
2. Printing Press	B. Evangelista Torricelli
3. Practical Batteries	C. Volta
4. Barometer	D. Edward Jenner

The correct links are 1-D, 2-A, 3-C and 4-B.

Section 2: Modern Marvels

Sub-section 2.1: 20th-Century Revolutionaries

In the 20th century, science flourished with breakthroughs from every corner of the globe.

What is radium?

860. That's the radioactive stuff Marie Curie dug up for its radioactive properties. She won two Nobel Prizes for her effort.

861. Hollywood actress Heddy Lamarr and composer George Antheil developed a frequency hopping technique that became the backbone of today's Wi-Fi and Bluetooth connectivity.

862. Albert Einstein was a 'God of Physics.' You know how important his work on relativity is, among many other contributions.

863. Nikola Tesla was a brilliant Serbian-American engineer who gave us alternating current.

864. Thomas Edison and Tesla were locked in a scientific and business battle known as the 'Battle of Currents.'

865. Edison wanted the world to use Direct Current, DC, while Tesla pushed for Alternating Current, AC.

866. Speaking of ACs, Willis Carrier invented the first practical air conditioning system in 1902. Cool!

867. During World War II, German forces communicated using secret codes on Enigma machines. Alan Turing broke the codes and that allowed the Allies to win the war.

868. Enrico Fermi built the first nuclear reactor known as the Chicago-Pile 1, CP1.

869. Lise Meitner discovered nuclear fission but was denied a Nobel prize due to prejudice.

Have you heard of Robert Oppenheimer?

870. J. Robert Oppenheimer led the Manhattan Project that developed the atomic bomb.

871. On June 6 and 9, 1945, the US dropped atomic bombs on the Japanese cities of Hiroshima and Nagasaki during World War II.

872. The two bombs, code-named Little Boy and Fat Man, led to Japan surrendering and ended the war.

873. The 2023 Hollywood blockbuster, Oppenheimer, was based on the life of Robert Oppenheimer.

How many people died from the atomic bombs?

874. The atomic bombs led to the death of an estimated 120,000 people and 73,000 people in Hiroshima and Nagasaki respectively in the first few days. Many more died from radioactive poisoning in later days.

875. Max Planck founded quantum theory and introduced the idea of quanta.

876. Neils Bohr developed the Bohr Model of the atom and advanced quantum mechanics theory.

877. Lise also helped to discover a radioactive element, protactinium and Einstein once referred to her as the German Marie Curie.

878. Grace Hopper, an American, invented the first computer compiler and coined the term 'debugging.'

879. In the 1950s, Jonas Salk developed the first effective polio vaccine.

880. In 1983, Sally Ride went into space as the first American woman to do so as part of the STS-7 crew. Groundbreaking!

881. In June 1963, Valentina Tereshkova, became the first woman to travel to space.

882. James Watson and Francis Crick shed light on DNA structure AND their findings of a double helix structure holds true today,

883. On July 21, 1969, history was made as Neil Armstrong stepped out of the Apollo 11 lunar module to become the first person to step on the surface of the moon.

Who was the second person on the moon?

884. Buzz Aldrin was the moon's second human visitor. He is also a retired astronaut and engineer.

885. Rachel Carson wrote one of the most significant books in recent memory, *Silent Spring*. The book sparked a resurgence of interest in the environment.

886. Linus Pauling won two Nobel Prizes - one for Peace and the other in Chemistry for his work on vitamins and nuclear disarmament

887. Using X-ray crystallography, Dorothy Hodgkin discovered the structure of penicillin and insulin.

888. Alexander Fleming discovered penicillin by mistake. Penicillin has saved millions of people from bacterial infections.

889. Konrad Lorenz, a Nobel laureate, is considered the 'Father of Ethology.' He studied animal behavior and bonding extensively and won the Nobel Prize in 1973.

890. Barbara McClintock discovered transposable elements after working with maize. At the time, her findings ran contrary to popular beliefs but she stuck to them and was proven right.

891. Frederick Sanger was a British biochemist who won two Nobel Prizes in Chemistry, the only person to do so.

892. In 1958, Sanger received his initial Nobel Prize for uncovering the amino acid sequence of insulin.

893. Sanger won his second Nobel Prize 22 years later in 1980 for his discoveries about DNA sequencing.

Who discovered the structure of antibodies?

894. In the late 1950s, Gary Edelman and Rodney Porter independently discovered the structure of antibodies. They shared the Nobel Peace prize in 1972 for Physiology/Medicine.

Interactive Activity: Who Did What?

Which notable 20th century scientist:

A. Led the Manhattan project

B. Won two Nobel Prizes in chemistry

C. Discovered the first polio vaccine

D. Built the first nuclear reactor?

The answers are Robert Oppenheimer, Frederick Sanger, Jonas Salk and Enrico Fermi in that order.

Sub-section 2.2: Contemporary Innovators

Today's scientists continue to break barriers and innovate across borders.

895. Elon Musk is a leading space explorer. He owns Space X and is on a mission to land on Mars.

896. Musk also owns Tesla, the leading American electric vehicles maker.

897. Katalin Kariko's mRNA vaccine theory was once mocked but it is still saving lives today.

898. Boyan Slat is using nets to attempt to clean up the oceans.

899. Jennifer Doudna is regarded as the CRISPR gene-editing queen for her work on genetics.

900. Dr. Mae Jemison, the inaugural African-American woman in space, passionately supports science education. Impressive!

901. Hadiyah-Nicole Green developed a laser treatment for cancer.

902. Temple Grandin is an autism advocate and designed humane systems for handling livestock.

903. Maryam Mirzakhani is the first woman to win the Fields Medal, mathematics' top prize. She is from Iran.

904. Tu YuYou from China developed a malaria treatment that has been saving a lot of lives.

905. Frances Arnold won a Nobel Prize for using evolution to design enzymes.

906. Andrea Ghez is credited with discovering a supermassive blackhole at the center of our universe.

907. Subrahmanyan Chandrasekhar explained how stars collapse into black holes

908. Donna Strickland, a Canadian, earned a Nobel Prize for her work on laser technology.

909. James Hansen was one of the first voices to warn about climate change in the 1980s. Foresight!

910. Elizabeth Blackburn was responsible for the discovery of telomeres. Telomeres affect aging in humans.

911. Gitanjali Rao is a young scientist recognized for her discovery of a device that can detect lead in water.

912. Shinya Yamanaka of Japan discovered how to turn adult cells into stem cells.

913. Dr Sarah Gilbert was the leader of the team that created the Oxford-AstraZeneca vaccine for COVID19.

914. Temnit Gebru is at the forefront of AI ethics and research to fight bias.

915. Bill Gates, the co-founder of Microsoft, is a philanthropist towards global health, education, and technology causes.

916. Antony Fauci is a leading expert on infectious diseases and he led the US response to Covid-19.

917. Yuval Noah Harari is an historian and the author of *Sapiens*. He explores human history to seek answers for the future.

918. Angela Merkel is a former German chancellor but she also has a PhD in quantum chemistry and is a passionate science advocate.

919. Demis Hassabis, a British AI researcher, co-founder, and CEO of DeepMind, developed AlphaGo.

920. In 2020, Hassabis and John Jumper also introduced a new AI tool that could present the structure of all known proteins. They named the tool AlphaFold 2.

921. Grid cells present in the brains of animals helped to understand space. It was May-Britt Moser who discovered the existence of these grid cells and he won a Nobel Prize for it.

922. In 1995, the Nobel Prize was given to Christiane Nusslein-Volhard, a geneticist who studied the development of fruit flies.

923. Sandra Faber, an American Professor of astronomy and astrophysics, is partly responsible for the Faber-Jackson equation and Keck telescopes.

Did you know that humans have explored Saturn?

924. Carolyn Porco is a planetary scientist with a lot of experience on space missions. She guided the imaging science team for the Cassini mission to Saturn, enhancing space science.

You know about Alibaba, the e-commerce giant, right?

925. Jack Ma is the man behind the Alibaba brand. He has contributed a lot to e-commerce and technology.

Jeff Bezos is popular with Amazon. But did you know that he also owns a space exploration company?

926. Yes! Bezos owns Blue Origin, a space exploration company. For a princely sum, you can ride with the company to space on a spaceship.

927. Sergey Brin and Larry Page are the names behind Google.

928. By creating the most powerful search engine ever, Brin and Page transformed information access.

929. Google also has a lot of other cool stuff like Google Maps for directions, Play Store for apps, and Gmail for your email needs.

930. Mark Zuckerberg created Facebook (now known as Meta) and has helped to shape social media and connectivity.

931. Meta also owns other platforms like Instagram, Whatsapp, and Oculus VR (now Meta Quest).

932. Satoshi Nakamoto is the unknown creator of Bitcoin, the top cryptocurrency.

Here is the most interesting part about Nakamoto!

933. Nobody knows who Satoshi Nakamoto is. Several people have been suspected of being Nakamoto including Hal Finney, Dorian Nakamoto, Nick Szabo and Craig Wright.

Interactive Activity: Who Owns What?

Which contemporary entrepreneur or innovator owns or is a co-founder of:

A. Instagram

B. Alibaba

C. Blue Origin

The right answers are:

A. Mark Zuckerberg (through Meta),

B. Jack Ma.

C. Jeff Bezos.

Sub-section 2.3: The Future of Global Innovation

The next generation of inventors is already shaping our future.

Young innovators are solving some of the world's biggest challenges, from climate change to healthcare. They bring fresh ideas and creativity to STEM fields.

934. We discussed Gitanjali Rao in the last subsection. Using nanotechnology to detect contaminants in water earned her Time magazine's first-ever "Kid of the Year" award in 2020.

What are some future technologies being developed by young innovators?

935. Young innovators are working on everything from AI-powered robots to eco-friendly inventions.

936. A group of students in Kenya created a solar-powered water purification system for their village.

937. Some young inventors have even started their own companies, like Boyan Slat, who founded The Ocean Cleanup to remove plastic from the ocean.

938. The NASA Space Apps Challenge invites kids from around the world to create solutions for space exploration and Earth's challenges.

939. Kelvin Doe, a Sierra Leonean, became popular for teaching himself engineering as a kid. He improvised and built his own mini radio station (from junk) under the name DJ Focus.

940. MIT invited Kelvin Doe to participate in the "Visiting Practitioner's" program. Kelvin became the youngest participant.

941. Ann Makosinski developed the thermoelectric flashlight, which converts heat from the palm of the user to electricity.

942. Makosinski also invented the eDrink Coffee mug, which also converts heat from the palm into electricity.

943. Easton LaChappelle may be young but he is making waves in the field of robotics. As a kid, he built a robotic hand that was controlled by his headset. He is also the Founder and CEO of "Unlimited Tomorrow."

What inventions does the future hold for us? What new challenges can we solve?

944. AI-doctors could become a more common thing. Robots and AI already have a role in diagnosis and even surgeries.

945. Scientists are already growing meat in labs to save animals and the planet.

946. Companies like SpaceX and Blue Origin are making space travel safe and available to everyone. Care for a ride into space? Strap up!

947. We already have smart, self-driving cars, solar roads, and AI recycling. Could we see entirely-smart cities very soon?

948. It is very likely that super-fast trains in vacuum tubes, traveling at 700 mph, could be the next advancement in traveling.

949. Wearable tech like smartwatches already exist to monitor our health. Could we see smart clothes soon, too?

950. Several scientists are involved in research into brain-computer interfaces. These are attempts to create devices that let us control computers with our minds.

951. Machines, like the ones built by Climeworks, attempt to battle climate change by sucking carbon dioxide out of the air directly.

952. Holograms will definitely be heavily involved in media exchange. These are 3D images that we can touch and interact with.

953. Space mining is a growing field that seeks to find precious metals from asteroids.

954. Tombot puppies from the Index project are examples of realistic robotic pets. These pets are built to mimic real pets but they don't need food or drink.

955. We already have Google Translate, but could we see universal translators that allow us to speak in any language we want?

956. Hydrogen fuel cells may be the energy source of the future. It is clean and reduces emissions.

957. Vertical farming utilizes vertically stacked layers to cultivate crops, effectively conserving space and water. This approach could be a solution for regions with dense populations.

Interactive Insight: Future Innovators Challenge

Imagine you could invent something to solve a global problem. What would it be? Create an illustration or describe your invention, then share it with friends or family.

Section 3: Inventions That Transcend Borders

Sub-section 3.1: Universal Technologies

Some inventions belong to all of humanity. Some inventions changed the course of science, culture and history. Some shaped the world for centuries to come.

Why was the invention of the printing press so important?

958. In the 15th century, Johannes Gutenberg developed the printing press, drawing inspiration from Chinese block printing techniques.

959. Before the printing press, books were painstakingly handwritten and priced so high that only the wealthy could afford them. Gutenberg's innovation transformed this reality, facilitating the global dissemination of knowledge and ideas.

Who invented the telephone?

960. In 1876, Alexander Graham Bell was recognized as the inventor of the telephone. His invention allowed people to communicate over long distances for the first time.

961. The first words conveyed through a telephone were, "Mr. Watson, come here.—I want to see you." The words were spoken by Graham Bell to his assistant, Thomas Watson, on March 10, 1876.

What is the internet and how did it start?"

962. The Internet is a global network of computers enabling instant information sharing among people.

963. The internet started as a military project in the 1960s and grew into the World Wide Web in the 1990s.

964. Tim Berners-Lee, a British scientist, invented the World Wide Web in 1989. He made it free for everyone to use, which helped it spread rapidly.

What is the significance of the light bulb?

965. The light bulb, perfected by Thomas Edison in 1879, revolutionized daily life by providing a reliable source of light. It allowed people to work and study after dark.

966. Edison tested over 6,000 materials before finding the right filament for his light bulb. His persistence finally paid off though!

967. In 1896, Guglielmo Marconi sent the first radio signals and he was issued a patent for his work in England.

968. Philo Farnsworth takes the credit for inventing the television in 1927. The first image to be transmitted was a straight line.

969. Joseph Nicéphore Niépce took the first photograph from a camera in 1826. Today, we have the most amazing cameras.

970. Steve Jobs unveiled the iPhone in 2007, transforming communication forever.

971. The Global Positioning System was developed for military use but it has now found use in several other ways.

972. Magnetic Resonance Imaging (MRI) was developed by Raymond Damadian and others in the 1970s. MRI is now a powerful tool in medicine.

973. There is some confusion about who invented it first, but Zacharias Jensen is often credited with inventing the first compound microscope.

974. Wilhelm Röntgen discovered X-rays by accident in 1895.

975. Theodore Maiman built the first working laser around 1960.

976. Igor Sikorsky made the first true helicopter in 1939 and flew it.

977. In 1835, Robert Andersen built an electric carriage powered by crude oil. That was the ancestor of current electric cars like Tesla and BYD.

978. The satellite Sputnik 1 was the first human-made object to enter Earth's orbit.

979. Sputnik 1 weighed 83 kg and was launched into space by the USSR in 1957.

980. The Jet Engine was developed in the 1930s by Frank Whittle and Hans von Ohain.

981. Karl Drais invented the bicycle in 1817 in Germany. He called his invention 'raisienne' or the 'running machine.'

What happens when scientists from all over the world join their efforts together? Great projects! What are some of these projects?

982. The International Space Station represents a partnership among the US, Russia, Europe, Japan, and other nations, allowing astronauts to work together in space.

983. The Large Hadron Collider is a European project with global participation in the field of particle physics.

984. The Human Genome Project represented a worldwide effort to chart the human genome.

985. The Montreal Protocol is a global pact designed to safeguard the ozone layer by fostering collaborative scientific initiatives.

986. The ITER project is an international collaboration aimed at advancing fusion energy, involving multiple nations.

987. Weather satellites are the bedrock of an international network for weather forecasting, and they also help global disaster preparedness.

988. There are global navigation satellite systems (GNSS): including GPS, GLONASS, and Galileo.

989. The World Health Organization (WHO) leads international health initiatives, such as combating pandemics.

990. The United Nations Educational, Scientific, and Cultural Organization (UNESCO) is a body for promoting science and culture internationally.

991. The International Astronomical Union (IAU) sets standards for astronomical nomenclature and global collaboration.

992. The International Council for Science (ICSU) coordinates scientific activity worldwide, fostering collaboration.

993. The Intergovernmental Panel on Climate Change (IPCC) evaluates scientific findings and advancements related to climate change.

994. The Convention on Biological Diversity (CBD) serves as a global pact focusing on the conservation of biodiversity and promoting scientific collaboration.

995. The International Space Exploration Coordination Group coordinates space exploration efforts among nations, like the Artemis program.

Interactive Activity: What's the Next Big Global Project?

I want you to brainstorm a bit. What current global challenge would benefit from collaboration among different countries? What approaches do you think will make the collaboration successful? Write down your ideas!

Sub-section 3.2: How Culture Shapes Innovation

Cultural diversity fuels creative solutions.

996. The drug aspirin was inspired by the use of willow bark in traditional medicine by Native Americans and ancient Greeks

What is the role of collaboration in global innovation?

997. Collaboration allows scientists from different cultures to share ideas and resources, leading to faster and more creative solutions.

998. Many scientific terms, like 'algorithm' and 'algebra,' come from Arabic, showing how cultures influence each other.

999. Many inventions are inspired by cultural needs. For example, the Japanese invented the bullet train to solve transportation problems in their crowded cities.

1000. The bullet train, or Shinkansen, can reach speeds of up to 200 miles per hour.

1001. Certain Asian communities use bamboo architecture for sustainable building.

1002. Many of the world's greatest inventions, like the compass, paper, and gunpowder, were first developed in China and later spread to the rest of the world.

1003. Herbal medicine from Africa, India and China have influenced modern pharmaceuticals.

1004. The Nobel Prize is presented each year to honor contributions in science, literature, and peace. It is named after Alfred Nobel, who invented dynamite.

Interactive Activity: Culture and Creativity Brainstorm

Think of a problem in your community. How can you use ideas from another culture to solve it? Write down your ideas and share them with a friend.

Chapter Takeaways

- From ancient innovators like Imhotep and Zhang Heng to modern pioneers like Marie Curie and Mae Jemison, global scientists have changed the world.
- Technological advancements like the printing press, telephone, and internet have connected people worldwide and transformed daily life.
- Cultural diversity fuels creativity and innovation, leading to breakthroughs in science and technology.
- Today's scientists are solving challenges in AI, health, and sustainability.
- The future belongs to young innovators who dare to dream.

Conclusion: Your Global STEM Adventure Continues

What an incredible, fun-filled journey we've shared! We've explored the wonders of science, technology, engineering, and math (STEM) through a kaleidoscope of facts, experiments, and stories from around the globe. Let's embark on a brief journey through our memories.

Cosmic Wonders introduced you to the universe's secrets—stars, galaxies, and the tools we use to study them. You met astronomers like Edwin Hubble and learned how ancient cultures mapped the skies.

Earth's Dynamic Landscape showed how volcanoes, earthquakes, and shifting tectonic plates shape our planet. We even explored how global scientists predict natural disasters.

Oceanic Mysteries plunged you into the deep blue, where glowing jellyfish, coral reefs, and cutting-edge submersibles revealed a world as vast as outer space.

Microcosm Magic zoomed into the tiny universe of cells, DNA, and microbes, proving that even the smallest life forms hold colossal power.

Forces Unleashed unraveled the invisible laws of physics—gravity, energy, and quantum weirdness—that make everything from roller coasters to smartphones possible.

Everyday STEM Adventures turned kitchens and backyards into labs, where baking soda volcanoes and homemade telescopes made science feel like play.

Digital Intelligence revealed how AI, like ChatGPT, learns, creates, and connects us across languages and cultures.

Global Innovators honored pioneers from every corner of the Earth, from ancient inventors to modern trailblazers like Mae Jemison and Fei-Fei Li.

All the chapters wove together over 1,000 facts, showing how science is not just a subject but a story of curiosity, creativity, and collaboration. One of the most exciting lessons from this book is how multicultural perspectives and advanced technologies work together to shape our world. Think about it! Ancient Babylonian astronomers mapped the stars, while Mayan mathematicians invented the concept of zero. Today, scientists from Nigeria to Norway use satellites and AI to solve global challenges.

Science isn't just about equations or lab coats—it's about people. It's about a kid in Kenya building a solar-powered water filter, a student in India coding a health app, or a team in Brazil protecting rainforests with drones. When we blend ideas from different cultures, we create better, brighter solutions for everyone.

Your Turn!!!

Here's the best part! You are now part of this story. Every fact you've learned, every experiment you've tried, and every question you've asked connects you to a worldwide community of explorers, thinkers, and dreamers.

Did you know that the ink in your pen, the screen on your tablet, and the Wi-Fi connecting you to friends across the globe all exist because someone, somewhere, asked "what if...?"

It is now your turn to ask "what if" questions everywhere and anywhere you go. Let curiosity guide your interest. Ask the difficult questions. Find solutions to problems. Dare to dream big!

The next great invention could start with your notebook, your curiosity, and a little backyard experiment.

Now that you've journeyed through the cosmos, Earth's depths, the microscopic world, and beyond, I have to ask "what will you create next?"

- Will you design a solution for heavy traffic?
- Could you invent a new way to grow food in space?
- Maybe you'll write code that helps people learn in 10 languages—or discover a species no one's ever seen!

There is absolutely nothing stopping you from doing these or any other things you have in mind.

Remember, science isn't just about 'right answers.' It's about asking bold questions, making messy mistakes, and learning from them. Let your experiments, creativity, and multicultural insights shape a brighter future.

Do not forget to join international science clubs like FIRST Robotics or UNESCO's Youth Climate Network. Remember to share your discoveries, too —start a STEM blog, film a TikTok experiment, or enter a science fair. Get up every day ready to explore! Be ready to achieve your own "eureka" moment!

As you close this book, remember that STEM isn't a destination—it's a journey. So grab your curiosity, your courage, and your sense of wonder. The future is yours to engineer, discover, and dream within.Go out there and make it amazing!

On your marks! Get set!! Eurekaaaaaa!!!

Special Bonus

Thank you for taking the time to read my book! We are delighted to offer the PDF of "Incredibly Interesting Global Facts For Smart Kids" free of charge.

https://pubbooklist.com/sci-fact

Readers have reported the following side effects:

- Uncontrollable Smiling – reacting to every friendly "hello" from across the globe!
- Joyful Tears – inspired by ancient landmarks revealing their hidden tales!
- A Spontaneous Urge to Explore – as the world calls you!
- Desire for Global Flavors – your kitchen can become a cultural center!
- Time-Traveling Fantasies – every chapter takes you on a journey through history!

Enjoy your complimentary sample audiobook!

Would you like a FREE copy of "**Incredibly Interesting Science Facts For Smart Kids**"? Find it below.

https://youtu.be/oW_Lj8cIqXI

If you're interested in the full audiobook, please refer to the information below or reach out to me directly via email.

https://pubbooklist.com/sci-fact

kate@pubbooklist.com

Thank You

If you enjoy our brand, be sure to check out our brand page for more exciting content!

https://www.amazon.com/stores/author/B0CKVJYFDB

You had many books to choose from, yet you selected this one—thank you! I truly appreciate your commitment to reading it thoroughly. Before you leave, I have a small request: could you please write a review on the platform? Your review is one of the simplest and most effective ways to support independent authors like me. Your insights will help me develop books that can aid you in achieving your goals. Hearing from you truly means a lot.

US: https://www.amazon.com/review/create-review/?asin=B0F2H3CYCF

UK: https://www.amazon.co.uk/review/create-review/?asin=B0F2H3CYCF

CA: https://www.amazon.ca/review/create-review/?asin=B0F2H3CYCF

References

1. AI Explorers - https://www.create-learn.us/ai-explorers
2. A Brief History of Time: From the Big Bang to Black Holes by Stephen Hawking (1988). Bantam Books. 3. Aurora: What Is an Aurora? - https://spaceplace.nasa.gov/aurora/en/
4. BioEd Online - https://www.bioedonline.org/
5. Black Holes - https://www.nationalgeographic.com/science/article/black-holes
6. British Geological Survey: Make-a-Map - https://www.bgs.ac.uk/discovering-geology/maps/make-a-geological-map/
7. CDC - The Human Microbiome - https://www.cdc.gov/genomics/disease/microbiome.htm
8. Canvas for Kids - https://www.create-learn.us/design-for-kids/graphic-design-canva
9. Clean Hands Knock Out Germs! - https://www.bioedonline.org/lessons-and-more/lessons/clean-hands-knock-out-germs/
10. CERN - The Large Hadron Collider - https://home.cern/science/accelerators/large- hadron-collider
11. Climate Change - https://www.nationalgeographic.com/environment/article/climate- change
12. Common Sense Education - https://www.commonsense.org/education/lists/terrific- websites-for-science
13. CONCEPT BUILDERS - https://www.physicsclassroom.com/Concept-Builders
14. Cosmos by Carl Sagan (1980). Random House. 15. Create & Learn - https://www.create-learn.us/ai-for-kids
16. Create with ChatGPT - https://www.create-learn.us/create-with-chatgpt
17. CRISPR Gene Editing - https://www.nature.com/articles/d41586-019-03919-0
18. DKfindout! - https://www.dkfindout.com/us/
19. Deep-Sea Creatures - https://www.nationalgeographic.com/animals/article/deep-sea- creatures
20. Discovery Education - https://www.discoveryeducation.com/solutions/science/
21. Earthquakes - https://www.usgs.gov/natural-hazards/earthquake-hazards
22. Encyclopedia Britannica - Isaac Newton - https://www.britannica.com/biography/Isaac-Newton
23. Encyclopedia Britannica - The History of AI - https://www.britannica.com/technology/artificial-intelligence
24. Encyclopedia Britannica - The History of Astronomy - https://www.britannica.com/science/astronomy
25. Encyclopedia Britannica - The History of Physics - https://www.britannica.com/science/physics
26. Encyclopedia Britannica - The Printing Press - https://www.britannica.com/technology/printing-press
27. Encyclopedia Britannica - The Theory of Relativity - https://www.britannica.com/science/theory-of-relativity
28. European Space Agency (ESA) - Cosmic Distances - https://www.esa.int/Science_Exploration/Space_Science/Cosmic_distances
29. Europa: Jupiter's Ocean World - https://spaceplace.nasa.gov/europa/en/
30. Full Moons: What Are the Different Types of Full Moons? - https://spaceplace.nasa.gov/full-moons/en/
31. Future of AI in Education - https://www.nationalgeographic.com/science/article/future- of-ai-in-education
32. Future of AI in Medicine - https://www.nationalgeographic.com/science/article/future- of-ai-in-medicine
33. Future of AI in Space Exploration - https://www.nationalgeographic.com/science/article/future-of-ai-in-space-exploration
34. Future of Artificial Intelligence - https://www.nationalgeographic.com/science/article/future-of-artificial-intelligence
35. Future of Biotechnology - https://www.sciencedaily.com/news/plants_animals/biotechnology/
36. Future of Genetic Engineering - https://www.nature.com/articles/d41586-019-03919-0
37. Future of Quantum Computing - https://www.nature.com/articles/d41586-021-00533-x
38. Future of Renewable Energy - https://www.nationalgeographic.com/environment/article/future-of-renewable-energy
39. Future of Robotics - https://www.nationalgeographic.com/science/article/future-of- robotics

40. Future of Space Exploration - https://www.nationalgeographic.com/science/article/future-of-space-exploration
41. Future of Space Travel - https://www.nationalgeographic.com/science/article/future-of- space-travel
42. Galileo Galilei - https://airandspace.si.edu/stories/editorial/galileo-galilei
43. Generation Genius - https://www.generationgenius.com/science-videos-for-kids/
44. Geological Society of London - https://www.geolsoc.org.uk/KS2Resources
45. Gravity and Relativity - https://www.nasa.gov/audience/forstudents/k-4/stories/nasa-knows/what-is-gravity-k4.html
46. Hubble Space Telescope - https://www.nasa.gov/mission_pages/hubble/main/index.html
47. Hubble's Law and the Expanding Universe - https://www.nasa.gov/mission_pages/hubble/science/hubble-law.html
48. Human Body - https://www.nationalgeographic.com/science/article/human-body
49. Human Genome Project - https://www.nature.com/articles/d41586-019-03166-3
50. International Space Station - https://www.nasa.gov/mission_pages/station/main/index.html
51. James Webb Space Telescope - https://www.jwst.nasa.gov/
52. Large Hadron Collider - https://home.cern/science/accelerators/large-hadron-collider
53. Make a Colorful Crayon Europa! - https://spaceplace.nasa.gov/europa-texture-coloring-activity/en/
54. Marie Curie and Radioactivity - https://www.nasa.gov/audience/forstudents/k- 4/stories/nasa-knows/who-was-marie-curie-k4.html
55. Mars 2020 Mission - https://mars.nasa.gov/mars2020/
56. Mars Rovers (Curiosity and Perseverance) - https://mars.nasa.gov/msl/home/ and https://mars.nasa.gov/mars2020/
57. McDonald Observatory - https://mcdonaldobservatory.org/teachers/classroom
58. Microbes - https://www.nationalgeographic.com/science/article/microbes
59. Microbiome - https://www.nature.com/articles/d41586-019-02807-x
60. MicroMatters: Microbiology - https://www.bioedonline.org/lessons-and-more/resource-collections/micromatters-microbiology/
61. MINDS ON PHYSICS - VERSION 5 - https://www.physicsclassroom.com/mop
62. Milky Way Galaxy - https://www.nationalgeographic.com/science/article/milky-way
63. MULTIMEDIA PHYSICS STUDIOS - https://www.physicsclassroom.com/mmedia
64. Mystery Science - https://mysteryscience.com/
65. NASA - Artificial Intelligence in Space Exploration - https://www.nasa.gov/feature/artificial-intelligence-in-space-exploration
66. NASA - Artemis Program - https://www.nasa.gov/specials/artemis/
67. NASA - Apollo Moon Landing - https://www.nasa.gov/mission_pages/apollo/index.html
68. NASA - Big Bang Theory - https://science.nasa.gov/astrophysics/focus-areas/what- powered-the-big-bang
69. NASA - Future of Space Exploration - https://www.nasa.gov/topics/future/index.html
70. NASA - Gravity and Relativity - https://www.nasa.gov/audience/forstudents/k- 4/stories/nasa-knows/what-is-gravity-k4.html
71. NASA - Hubble Space Telescope - https://www.nasa.gov/mission_pages/hubble/main/index.html
72. NASA - James Webb Space Telescope - https://www.jwst.nasa.gov/
73. NASA - Mars 2020 Mission - https://mars.nasa.gov/mars2020/
74. NASA - Mars Rovers (Curiosity and Perseverance) - https://mars.nasa.gov/msl/home/ and https://mars.nasa.gov/mars2020/
75. NASA - New Horizons Mission to Pluto - https://www.nasa.gov/mission_pages/newhorizons/main/index.html
76. NASA - Parker Solar Probe - https://www.nasa.gov/parker-solar-probe
77. NASA - Search for Exoplanets - https://exoplanets.nasa.gov/
78. NASA - Search for Life Beyond Earth - https://www.nasa.gov/astrobiology/
79. NASA - Solar System Exploration - https://solarsystem.nasa.gov/
80. NASA - Voyager Missions - https://voyager.jpl.nasa.gov/
81. National Geographic - Albert Einstein - https://www.nationalgeographic.com/science/article/albert-einstein
82. National Geographic - Ancient Innovations - https://www.nationalgeographic.com/history/article/ancient-innovations

83. National Geographic - Black Holes -
https://www.nationalgeographic.com/science/article/black-holes
84. National Geographic - Climate Change -
https://www.nationalgeographic.com/environment/article/climate-change
85. National Geographic - Deep-Sea Creatures -
https://www.nationalgeographic.com/animals/article/deep-sea-creatures
86. National Geographic - Future of AI in Education -
https://www.nationalgeographic.com/science/article/future-of-ai-in-education
87. National Geographic - Future of AI in Medicine -
https://www.nationalgeographic.com/science/article/future-of-ai-in-medicine
88. National Geographic - Future of AI in Space Exploration -
https://www.nationalgeographic.com/science/article/future-of-ai-in-space-exploration
89. National Geographic - Future of Artificial Intelligence -
https://www.nationalgeographic.com/science/article/future-of-artificial-intelligence
90. National Geographic - Future of Renewable Energy -
https://www.nationalgeographic.com/environment/article/future-of-renewable-energy
91. National Geographic - Future of Robotics -
https://www.nationalgeographic.com/science/article/future-of-robotics
92. National Geographic - Future of Space Exploration -
https://www.nationalgeographic.com/science/article/future-of-space-exploration
93. National Geographic - Future of Space Travel -
https://www.nationalgeographic.com/science/article/future-of-space-travel
94. National Geographic - History of the Internet -
https://www.nationalgeographic.com/history/article/history-of-the-internet
95. National Geographic - Human Body -
https://www.nationalgeographic.com/science/article/human-body
96. National Geographic - Microbes -
https://www.nationalgeographic.com/science/article/microbes
97. National Geographic - Milky Way Galaxy -
https://www.nationalgeographic.com/science/article/milky-way
98. National Geographic - Plate Tectonics -
https://www.nationalgeographic.org/encyclopedia/plate-tectonics/
99. National Geographic - Solar System -
https://www.nationalgeographic.com/science/article/solar-system
100. National Geographic - Volcanoes -
https://www.nationalgeographic.com/environment/article/volcanoes
101. National Geographic Kids - https://kids.nationalgeographic.com/
102. Nature - CRISPR Gene Editing - https://www.nature.com/articles/d41586-019-03919-0
103. Nature - Future of Genetic Engineering - https://www.nature.com/articles/d41586-019-03919-0
104. Nature - Future of Quantum Computing - https://www.nature.com/articles/d41586-021-00533-x
105. Nature - Future of Space Travel - https://www.nature.com/articles/d41586-021-00533-x
106. Nature - History of AI - https://www.nature.com/articles/d41586-019-03013-5
107. Nature - Human Genome Project - https://www.nature.com/articles/d41586-019-03166- 3
108. Nature - Microbiome - https://www.nature.com/articles/d41586-019-02807-x
109. NOAA - Coral Reefs - https://oceanservice.noaa.gov/facts/coralreef-climate.html
110. NOAA - Deep Ocean - https://oceanservice.noaa.gov/facts/deep-ocean.html
111. NOAA - Ocean Cleanup Project - https://www.noaa.gov/education/resource- collections/ocean-coasts/ocean-pollution
112. NOAA - Ocean Exploration - https://oceanexplorer.noaa.gov/
113. NOAA - Ocean Exploration Technologies -
https://oceanexplorer.noaa.gov/technology/technology.html
114. NOAA - Role of AI in Climate Change - https://www.noaa.gov/stories/artificial-intelligence-and-climate-change
115. NOAA - Role of AI in Ocean Exploration -
https://oceanexplorer.noaa.gov/technology/ai/ai.html
116. NOAA - Role of AI in Weather Prediction - https://www.noaa.gov/stories/artificial-intelligence-improves-weather-forecasts

117. NOAA - Role of Satellites in Climate Monitoring - https://www.noaa.gov/education/resource-collections/climate/climate-monitoring
118. NOAA - Role of Satellites in Weather Forecasting - https://www.noaa.gov/education/resource-collections/weather-atmosphere/weather- satellites
119. OpenAI - ChatGPT - https://openai.com/blog/chatgpt
120. PBS KIDS for Parents - https://www.pbs.org/parents/learn-grow/all-ages/science
121. PHYSICS SIMULATIONS - https://www.physicsclassroom.com/Physics-Interactives
122. Python for AI - https://www.create-learn.us/coding-for-kids/python
123. Quantum Physics - https://www.sciencedaily.com/news/matter_energy/quantum_physics/
124. Renaissance Science - https://www.smithsonianmag.com/history/renaissance-science-180968314/
125. Science Daily - Future of AI in Medicine - https://www.sciencedaily.com/news/computers_math/artificial_intelligence/
126. Science Daily - Future of Biotechnology - https://www.sciencedaily.com/news/plants_animals/biotechnology/
127. Science Daily - Future of Quantum Computing - https://www.sciencedaily.com/news/matter_energy/quantum_computing/
128. Science Daily - Quantum Physics - https://www.sciencedaily.com/news/matter_energy/quantum_physics/
129. Science Journal for Kids - https://www.sciencejournalforkids.org/
130. Science News Explores - https://www.snexplores.org/
131. Silent Spring by Rachel Carson (1962). Houghton Mifflin. 132. Skywatching Tips - https://solarsystem.nasa.gov/skywatching/home/
133. Smithsonian Magazine - History of Earthquakes - https://www.smithsonianmag.com/science-nature/history-earthquakes-180968314/
134. Smithsonian Magazine - History of Science - https://www.smithsonianmag.com/history/history-science-180968314/
135. Smithsonian Magazine - Renaissance Science - https://www.smithsonianmag.com/history/renaissance-science-180968314/
136. Smithsonian National Air and Space Museum - Galileo Galilei - https://airandspace.si.edu/stories/editorial/galileo-galilei
137. Smithsonian Ocean - Marine Biodiversity - https://ocean.si.edu/ocean-life
138. Smithsonian Science Education Center - https://ssec.si.edu/
139. STEM@Home Activities - https://www.bioedonline.org/stem-home-activities/
140. THE PHYSICS CLASSROOM TUTORIAL - https://www.physicsclassroom.com/class
141. The Age of Wonder: How the Romantic Generation Discovered the Beauty and Terror of Science by Richard Holmes (2008). HarperPress.
142. The Code Book: The Science of Secrecy from Ancient Egypt to Quantum Cryptography by Simon Singh (1999). Anchor Books.
143. The Demon-Haunted World: Science as a Candle in the Dark by Carl Sagan (1995). Random House.
144. The Disappearing Spoon: And Other True Tales of Madness, Love, and the History of the World from the Periodic Table of the Elements by Sam Kean (2010). Little, Brown and Company.
145. The Double Helix: A Personal Account of the Discovery of the Structure of DNA by James D. Watson (1968). Atheneum.
146. The Elegant Universe: Superstrings, Hidden Dimensions, and the Quest for the Ultimate Theory by Brian Greene (1999). W.W. Norton & Company.
147. The Emperor of All Maladies: A Biography of Cancer by Siddhartha Mukherjee (2010). Scribner.
148. The Fabric of the Cosmos: Space, Time, and the Texture of Reality by Brian Greene (2004)

Printed in Dunstable, United Kingdom

67699488R00078